MIDDLE ENGLISH TEXTS/8

General Editor: M. GÖRLACH

MIDDLE ENGLISH TEXTS

HEIDELBERG 1978

CARL WINTER · UNIVERSITÄTSVERLAG

JULIAN OF NORWICH'S
REVELATIONS OF DIVINE LOVE

The Shorter Version

ed. from B.L. Add. MS 37790

by

FRANCES BEER

HEIDELBERG 1978

CARL WINTER · UNIVERSITÄTSVERLAG

CIP-Kurztitelaufnahme der Deutschen Bibliothek

Juliana ⟨of Norwich⟩
[Revelations of divine love]
Julian of Norwich's revelations of divine love:
the shorter version ed. from B. L. Add. MS 37790/
by Frances Beer. — Heidelberg: Winter, 1978.

(Middle English texts; 8)
Einheitssacht.: Sixteen revelation of divine love
ISBN 3-533-02692-2
NE: Beer, Frances [Hrsg.]

ISBN 3-533-02692-2

CONTENTS

Abbreviations and Acknowledgements   6

Introduction   7
  1 Biography   7
  2 Manuscripts
     a) The Shorter Version   9
     b) The Longer Version   12
  3 Language
     a) Morphology   14
     b) Phonology and Spelling   15
     c) Conclusion   18
  4 The Corrector   20
  5 Differences Between the Short and
     the Longer Versions   22
  6 The Relationship of the MSS   25
  7 Julian's Subject Matter   28
  8 Editorial Method   36

REVELATIONS OF DIVINE LOVE   39

Notes   81

Bibliography   99

ABBREVIATIONS

Manuscripts

A	British Library, Additional MS 37790 (Amherst)
P	Bibliothèque Nationale, Paris, Fonds anglais 40
S1	British Library MS Sloane 2499
S2	British Library MS Sloane 3705
	[When S1 and S2 agree they are cited as SS]

Other Works

Book	The Book of Privy Counselling
Cloud	The Cloud of Unknowing
Scale	The Scale of Perfection
Wohunge	Þe Wohunge of Ure Lauerd

EETS	Early English Text Society
MED	Middle English Dictionary
OED	Oxford English Dictionary

Works cited otherwise are identified by author or editor, and year of publication. Full references will be found in the Bibliography.

ACKNOWLEDGEMENTS

I would like to express my gratitude to a number of people who have offered helpful advice and criticism during the preparation of this edition: P.L. Heyworth, my thesis supervisor, M. Görlach and O.S. Pickering, the editors of this series, A. McIntosh and M. Laing, A. Cameron and A.G. Rigg. This edition began as a doctoral dissertation at the Centre for Medieval Studies, University of Toronto; thanks are also due to the Canada Council, the Province of Ontario, and Atkinson College, York University for funds granted during its preparation, and to the British Library Board for permission to reproduce a page from B.L. Additional MS 37790.

INTRODUCTION

1   Biography

The established facts of the life of Julian of Norwich are
few. We know that when she was "thryttye wyntere alde and a
halfe" (41/4) she suffered a near-fatal illness during which
she experienced the sixteen shewings described in the Revelations of Divine Love. The illness occurred in "the yer of
our lord a thousande and thre hundered and lxxiii the xiii
daie of may" (P f.3r; S1 and S2 give the date as May 8). This
would place Julian's birth date in the latter part of 1342.
The incipit of the Amherst version of the Revelations tells us
that Julian "ʒitt ys on lyfe" in 1413, and that she was a recluse at St. Julian's Church in Norwich. A reference in a
1416 will establishes that she was still alive in that year.[1]

There are two versions of the Revelations, a short and a long
one. Her first, shorter record of the shewings must have
been set down shortly after their occurrence, as the account
is so clear and detailed. Then, "twenty yere after the tyme
of the shewyng saue thre monthys" (P f.96v), Julian "had te-
chyng inwardly" that inspired the longer version; this version
contains the fruits of intervening meditation, "renewde by
lyghtenynges and touchynges" (P f.104v). While most of the
material from the earlier version is retained, there are some
interesting changes and additions that merit special consideration, and are discussed in section 5.

When Julian became a recluse,[2] or whether she was a religious,[3]

1   Jacob and Johnson (1937:II,95).

2   See Molinari (1958:7ff.), Blomefield (1805-10:II,546). The church
     to which Julian's anchorhold was attached belonged to the Benedictine
     nuns of Carrow; Julian may first have been part of that community,
     moving to their anchorhold when she became a recluse.

3   In Rye (1889:Appendix IX) nuns are listed as either Dame or
     Lady, but Julian is only referred to as a 'deuout woman'; on the
     other hand, Margery Kempe does call her "Dame Ielyan" (Meech
     1961:42). Colledge and Walsh (1975:417) conjecture that Julian
     "was a member of a community of contemplative nuns for some
     years before the revelations".

is not known. That she was not enclosed at the time of her
sickness is suggested by her own testimony: her mother and
friends were with her by her sick-bed (54/19), and her local
priest, "the person my curette" (41/29), was sent for when
she seemed at the point of death (cf. Reynolds 1956:xiii).

As an anchoress, however, the extent of her renown as a spiritual advisor is attested by the fact that her advice was sought
by Margery Kempe.[4] If Julian's words to Margery are typical,
this renown was apt. On the one hand, while urging Margery to
fulfill "what-euyr [God] put in her sowle", she adds the firm,
if tactful rider, "yf it wer not a-geyn þe worshep of God &
profyte of his euyn-cristen": God and her fellow Christians,
rather than herself, ought to be the focus of her love and attention.[5] On the particular distressing question of Margery's
cryings, Julian is able to offer reassurance. "Seynt Powyl
seyth þat þe Holy Gost...makyth vs to askyn & preyn wyth morn-
ynggys & wepyngys so plentyvowsly þat þe terys may not be nowm-
eryd", and "Ierom seyth þat terys turmentyn mor þe Devylle þan
don þe peynes of Helle". Finally she reminds Margery, and this
must have been enormously comforting to one so scorned, that
"þe mor despyte, schame, & repref þat 3e haue in þe world, þe
mor is 3owr meryte in the sygth of God".

Julian's tact and compassion seem the more extraordinary when
we consider how opposite were the women: Margery with her
white clothes and her roarings, Julian, enclosed, describing
herself only as a "symple creature vnlettyrde" (P f.3r), in-
sisting that the shewings reflect no special merit on her part;
"for the schewynge I am not goode but 3if y love god the better" (47/1); "it was nought schewyd vnto me for that god loves
me bettere thane the leste sawle that is in grace" (47/8-9).

That Julian was, in fact, "vnlettyrde", or "leued" as she elsewhere calls herself (48/2), is less than obvious. It may be

---

4   The Book of Margery Kempe, ed. Meech (1961:42-3).

5   "Þe Holy Gost", adds Julian with her characteristic good sense,
     "meuyth neuyr a þing a-geyn charity, &, yf he dede, he wer contraryows
     to hys owyn self, for he is al charite" (Meech 1961:42).

that she did not know Latin (Reynolds 1956:viii), or that she
herself could not read or write. But she must have been a
woman of some education. Her manner of expression itself establishes this: Reynolds draws particular attention to Julian's
use of a number of traditional rhetorical devices, such as
alliteration, synonymous phrases, repetition, and antithesis.[6]
Perhaps more impressive is the range of spiritual writers with
whose work she was apparently familiar: Rolle, Hilton, the au-
thors of The Cloud of Unknowing and Þe Wohunge of Ure Lauerd.[7]
That she was modest in the extreme seems the more likely explanation for her protestations of ignorance and unworthiness,
her argument that the shewings were not sent for her, but for
the comfort of all God's lovers:

> I praye ʒowe alle...that ʒe leve the behaldynge of the
> wrechid worldes synfulle creature that it was schewyd
> vnto, &...behalde god that of his curtays love and of
> his endles goodnes walde schewe generalye this visyon
> in comforthe of vs alle (46/21ff.).

2   Manuscripts

a)   The Shorter Version

The short text of Julian of Norwich's Revelations of Divine
Love, here edited, exists in one copy: the Amherst MS, B.L.
Additional MS 37790.[8] Acquired at the Amherst sale, Sotheby's,
24-27 March, 1910, lot 813, it bears the bookplates of William
Constable and Lord Amherst, as well as the monogram of James
Grenehalgh. The MS is an anthology of devotional pieces, per-
haps compiled for the use of a religious community. All but
one of the entries are in English.

The chief author represented is Richard Rolle, and the explicit
to his Fyre of lufe establishes 1435 as the terminus post quem

---

6   See Reynolds (1956:xxxviii ff.; 1958:xxii ff.); also Colledge
    and Walsh (1975:422ff.).

7   For specific parallels see the Notes, particularly to 40/33, 42/8ff.,
    43/12-3, 43/30-2, 49/1-2, 52/26ff., 54/30-2, 56/13, 58/23-4.

8   The Catalogue of Additions to the Manuscripts in the British Museum
    1906-10 (1912:153); see also Reynolds (1956:ii), Colledge and
    Bazire (1957:9, 83), Colledge and Walsh (1975:404).

of the MS.[9] The MS is vellum, originally consisting of 240 folios, measuring 209 x 136 mm. Text area is 147-153 mm. x 88-92mm., with 31-35 lines to the page. The MS appears to collate in eights.[10] Gatherings are numbered in the lower right hand corner; in addition, the folios are numbered in ink, in a modern hand. The text area is defined by vertical and horizontal rules; large blue capitals with red flourishes mark the textual divisions.

The hand of the Amherst scribe, clear and elegant, matches that described by Parkes[11] as Anglicana Formata. The letters are squarish, and carefully formed. In the letter m each minim is separate; the stroke between the head and the foot of the minim is relatively long and straight. Excluding the 'capital' form, the letter a is virtually the same height as the other letters, while the shaft of the t extends well above the head stroke. The 'capital' form of short s, and the short r, have been borrowed from the university book hands. Some Latin phrases (as 43/13, 45/28) are given prominence by use of a large textura script. I have underlined these words in the text.

The entire MS has been written by one scribe, but it appears to divide into three 'books', each of which contains one or more major entries, and is 'filled up' at the end by short excerpts:[12]

9   "Explicit liber de incendio amoris Ricardi Hampole heremite trans-
     latus in Anglicum instanciis domine Margarete Heslyngton recluse
     per fratrem Ricardum Misyn...anno domini millesimo ccccxxxv" (f.95r).

10   In the Julian extract the gatherings are numbered as follows :
     97r   n.1   105r   o.1   113r   p.1
     98r   n.2   106r   o.2   114r   p.2
     99r   n.3   107r   o.3   115r   p.3
     100r   n.4   108r   o.4
     101r-104r blank   109r-112r blank

11   Parkes (1969:xvi ff.).

12   The fact that some of the MS entries are excerpts, and that the
     MS was made well after the composition of the longer version,
     raises the possibility that the shorter version of the Revelations
     is itself an abridgement; this question is discussed in section 5.

...sse as it es to me. ffor this syght was schewyd in generalle & nathynge in specyalle. Of alle that I sawe this was the maste cõfortye to me that oure lorde es so hamlye & so curtayse And this maste ful fyld me with lykynge & sekernes in saule than sayde I to the folke that were with me itt es to daye domesdaye with me & this I say de for I wenede to hafe dyed for that daye that man or womann dy es ye he demyd as he schalle be with owttyn eende this I sayde for y walde thaye lowyd god mare & sette the lesse pryse be the vanite of the worlde forto make thame to hafe mynde that this lyfe es schorte as thaye myght se in ensampill be me. ffor in alle þis tyme y ... aftyr this I sawe with bodely syght (I nede to hafe dyed

the face of the crucifixe that hange before me in whilke I behelde cõtynuely a partye of his passyon despite spyttynge in solowynge of his bodye & buffetynge in his blyssfulle face & manye langonzes and paynes ma than I can telle and ofte chaungynge of colowre and alle his blyssede face Atyme closede in dry blode this I sawe bodylye & hevelye & derkelye and I desyred mare bodely syght to hafe sene more clerelye and I was answerde in my resone that if god walde schewe me mare he schulde botte me nedde na lyght bote hym and aftyr this I sawe god in a poynte that es in myne understã dynge. In whilke syght I sawe that he es in alle thynge I behelde with avysemente wittande and knawande in that syght that he do se alle that es done. I merveylede in this syght with a softe drede & thought whate es synne. ffor I sawe trulye that god dothe alle thyn ge be itt nevere so litille. nor nathynge es done be happe ne be eventure botte the endeles forsihe of the wysdome of god whare fore me behovede nedes graunte that alle thynge that es done es wele done and I was sekyr that god dose na synne was nouзt schewyd me and y walde no lengur mervelle of this botte behalde oure lorde whate he wolde schewe me & in Anothyr tyme god schewyd me whate synne es nakydlye be the selfe as y schalle telle aftyr warde and aftyr þis I sawe he hangand the rode plentewouslye bledande hate & freshe lyke and lufefye ryзt as I sawe before in the heede And this was sha wed

M y fore it semed to me þt synne is nouзt. ffor in all thys. synne

ff. 1r-96v   The Mendynge of lyfe (ff. 1r-19r)
             The Fyre of lufe (ff. 19v-95r)
             A goldyn pystille "[made by] Saynte Barnarde
             vnto his cosyn" (f. 96v)
ff. 97r-136v The Revelations of Divine Love (ff. 97r-115r)
             Tretesse of perfeccion of the sonnys of god,
             "compiled bi Dan Iohn Rusbroke...[translated]
             frome Latyn in to Englysch" (ff. 115r-130r)
             De triplici genere amoris spiritualis [Form of
             Living, chs. viii-x] (ff. 130v-131v)
             Tractatus de Diligendo deo [Form of Living, ch.
             vii], and Ego Dormio [an extract] (ff. 132r-136v)
             Formula compendiosa vite spiritualis [part of
             ch. iv of the abridged English version of Horo-
             logium Sapientiae] (f. 136v)
ff. 137r-240v Þe Myrroure of symple saules, "[translated] out
             of Frensch in to englisch" (ff. 137r-225r)
             Liber soliloquorum animae ad deum [in Latin];
             an English extract on three ways of contempla-
             tion; a short extract on penance; a brief note
             on the visions of St. Bridget (ff. 225v-238v)
             [last folio cut away]

The Amherst Revelations has been annotated by three different
readers, not including the corrector, who is discussed sepa-
rately in section 4. The marginalia of a neat, small, 15th-
century hand are confined to nota and nota bene. A 16th-century
annotator writes at the top of the first folio of the MS
"Vincit Winge his Booke"; he is given to underlining key words
(as contricion, confessyon, pennance), and copying them in the
margin. The hand of the third annotator, who also confines
his remarks to nota, is faint and undistinguished. The marginalia of these readers are of little interest, though the
fact that they centre around the discussions of sin (f. 108v)
and prayer (f.110r) may indicate that these were the passages
most frequently read.

b)   The Longer Version

The complete longer version of the Revelations is found in
three MSS: Bibliothèque Nationale, Paris, Fonds anglais 40,
dated in the B.N. Catalogue as 16th-century;[13] British Li-

---

13   Colledge and Walsh (1975:405) point out that "previous scholars...
     have been deceived...by the faked antique appearance of Fonds
     anglais 40 into calling it 'sixteenth century'; we shall describe
     it as...certainly of the seventeenth century, probably c. 1650".

brary MS Sloane 2499 of the mid-17th century; and B.L. MS
Sloane 3705 of the early 18th century. The earliest printed
edition, entitled Sixteen Revelations of Divine Love shewed
to a deuout servant of our Lord called Mother Juliana, an
Anchorete of Norwich: who lived in the Dayes of King Edward
the Third, was published in 1670 by the Benedictine Serenus
de Cressy. Its text follows that of the Paris MS very closely,
and was almost certainly taken from that copy.

Excerpts from the Revelations also appear in the early 16th-
century Westminster Cathedral Treasury MS 4 (f.72v ff.)[14] and
the 17th-century Upholland anthology located in St. Joseph's
College Library, Upholland, Lancashire (f. 113r ff.).[15] Westminster parallels P, although it rearranges the order; the extract blends portions of Revelations i, ii, iii, ix, x, xiv,
and chs. 41-64 of the longer version. Upholland includes Revelations xii and xiii, and portions of chs. 28, 30, and 32.
It follows both P and the 1670 Cressy text closely; it is
difficult to determine the direct source, as the Julian passages display some features found only in P, and some found only
in Cressy.

Of the three complete copies of the longer version, Reynolds,
after a full collation of the MSS, chooses P as her base text
because "the greater integrity of its text [suggests] that the
original of P was close to the text as it left Julian's hand
or that of her scribe" (1956:xvi ff.). Walsh points out that
the discovery of Westminster, as it regularly follows P,
substantiates Reynolds' conclusion.[16] Colledge and Walsh,
too, use P as the basis of their forthcoming edition of the
longer version. Glasscoe, on the other hand, bases her recent
edition on S1.[17]

---

14   See Foucard (1956:41-3) and Ker (1960:418).

15   Owen (1968:270ff.).

16   Walsh (1961:v).

17   Glasscoe (1976:viii): "S1 has been chosen as copy text...because
      its language is much closer to the 14th-century English than
      that of P."

3   Language

One might assume that the dialect of the Amherst Revelations
would be that of the Norfolk region; in fact, it shows marked
northern features, with scattered East Midlands characteristics. It could possibly be argued that Julian herself, or
her amanuensis, was from the North; the more likely explanation,
as an examination of the text suggests, is that the mixed nature of the language is the result of several stages of transmission.

a) Morphology

The morphological features of the Amherst Revelations are, in
general, northern. Nominative singular of the feminine pronoun divides evenly between scho and sche; 3rd plural pronoun,
both nominative and oblique, has initial th/þ (thaye, tham, th/
þayre). Substantive endings are unexceptional, with -es/-ys for
both genitive singular and nominative plural (but cf. criste 54/
15, wyntere 41/4, eyen 54/20; and colourse 53/24, hevens 57/5).

A's regular first person singular present indicative is -es
(cownsayles 46/22, loves 70/4); 3rd singular present indicative
ends in -s (as wyndes 43/30), and 2nd plural in -s, -es, or
-ys (hyerys, sees 46/27); 3rd plural present indicative ends
in -es/-s (sekes 45/14, offers 52/10). The plural imperative
form lacks final -th/þ (thynke 58/19), and the strong past par-
ticiples are in -en(e)/-n (chosene 50/30, byddyn 62/1). Final
-ande for the present participle is regular (prayande 40/30),
while verbal substantives are in -ynge (comfortynge 51/12,
buffettynge 49/17).[18]

The evidence presented by the verb 'to be', however, is less
conclusively northern.[19] Third singular present indicative
is es, is, ys; plural present indicative is er(e), ar(e);

---

18   Angus McIntosh and Margaret Laing, at work on the language of the
     Amherst Revelations, specify -es, -ys, -is, -s, -ez as 3rd sg. pres.
     ind. endings; in addition, they point out that, when the root ends
     in y, the verbal substantives end in -ing(e), ingge.

19   See Forsström (1948:92ff., 174ff.), who includes the Guild Records,
     the Paston Letters, and Kempe's Book in his discussion.

plural present subjunctive is be; plural preterite indicative
is ware, were. While these forms can be northern, all are
found in texts of the East Midlands as well. For 3rd singular
present indicative the 14th-century Norfolk Guild Records have
is, his, es; Margery Kempe uses is, the Paston Letters ys, is,
isse. For plural present indicative the Guilds use ben(e),
bien, but also arn, ere; Kempe uses ben, but also arn, the Pastons be. Plural present subjunctive be is common to all three;
for plural preterite indicative the Guilds use werin, weren,
Kempe and the Pastons wer(e). The Norfolk region, then, is
not excluded actively by this much of the evidence of the verb
'to be'.

Yet, while be(n) appears as a regular plural present indicative
East Midlands form, it does not occur in the Amherst Revelations; and, while ware and were for plural preterite indicative
were competing forms in the North, and appear with equal fre-
quency in the Amherst Revelations, ware is used neither by the
Guilds nor by Kempe.[20] In sum, then, the evidence of the verb
'to be' suggests the possibility, as do the other morphological
features, of a location somewhat to the north of Norfolk.

b) Phonology and Spelling

Phonological features of the language are also predominantly
northern. The reflex of OE /a:/ is usually spelled a (banes
54/6, anly 56/10, awe 62/20), but o forms are also found
(lothe 41/11, clothes 41/26); gastelye and gostelye appear in
a ratio of 10:1, mare and more in a ratio of 7:1. OE /al +
d/ appears regularly as ald (alde 41/4, calde 54/10; but cf.
tolde 54/13). The ratio between behalde and beholde is 6:1.

Before a nasal, a for OE /a/ is invariable, which excludes the
West Midlands (man 40/26, manye 49/17, thanke 51/21); and excluding both West Midlands and South, the reflex of OE /e:o/ is
spelled e (chese 56/1), and OE /y(:)/ appears as i/y (kyrke
39/19, kynde 42/22, drye 53/18). Besy and mery appear, but as
Bazire points out, the evolution of their vowels is governed by

20 Forsström (1948:206). The Paston Letters produce one war spelling
    in 31 examples.

the subsequent s or r, and they cannot be taken to illus-
trate the development of OE /y(:)/.[21]

In combination, the following forms would seem to point to the
North:[22] kyrke,[23] ilke, myrke, tylle ('to'), blude, sall(e)
(though blode and schalle are regular). On the other hand, the
text shows mixed evidence of voicing and unvoicing, especially
in the case of f/v: lefe and leve, safe and save both occur,
though safe is more common; lyffande/lyevande, lyflye/lyvelye,
luffe/love seem to be interchangeable. Again, some northern
influence is apparent, but the evidence continues to be mixed.

ȝ is used in several ways.[24] It is invariably used for /j/,
as in ȝonge 44/23, ȝit 63/12; in addition, it can represent
[ç] or [x] as myȝt (42/7), ryȝt (50/8) (myght and ryght are
regular), þowȝ (51/28), thouȝt (41/11) (thought is regular),
and tauȝt (47/32) (taught also occurs). Rarely, ȝ and gh are
combined (lughȝ 51/8); towards the end of the text ȝ is several
times used to indicate final s/z (doez 76/18; comonez 79/13).

Initially and medially th is usual; þ is used most often in
abbreviated forms, but also in words such as þat, þou, þare,
þis, þowȝ. Sch occurs initially, medially and finally. ff
and f seem interchangeable; ff is found most frequently in
ffor. For /v/, u and v appear to be used interchangeably
(deservede/deseruede; delyverede/delyuerede; ever/euer;
servyce/seruyce). Except where i stands for /dȝ/, i and y also
seem to be interchangeable, though the scribe shows a marked
preference for y, especially with minim groups. When i is
used with minims (as dyinge, enioyes, in), it is distinguished
by a superior mark.

---

21 Bazire (1957:65n). McIntosh and Laing remark that words with
   OE ȳ have "such differing developments...that one might as
   well admit that each word should be regarded differently",
   pointing specifically to A's furste (45/30).
22 See MED; Sisam (1967:276ff.); Mossé (1961:16ff.).
23 But cf. Samuels' map in Jones (1972:196).
24 Cf. Davis (1967:135-6).

Graphic reduplication of e̲ and o̲ can be used to indicate length,
as eelde (40/25), heede (42/16), woo (53/4); but both feendys
(43/25) and fendys (42/13) occur, as do leevyd (39/16) and beleve (39/21), s̈eekenes (40/18) and sekenes (40/9). I/y as a
sign of length is only rarely found (as feyndys 40/14, forsayke
60/3). Initial h̲- in a word of French origin is once omitted,
abylle (45/23) also spelled habelynge (69/19); usually h̲ is retained or added, as hesyd (61/15; ese is the usual form), huglye (42/12), also spelled vglye (60/24). Distinctive, too, are
forms in -ye-, such as lyeve, lyekenes, syeker, syekenes (lyffede, lyknes, sekere, sekenes are also found).[26]

Without McIntosh and Samuels' forthcoming Survey of Middle English Dialects, it is difficult to assess the graphemic evidence
and to ascertain whether the mixed data actually represent the
spelling of one scribe, or are the result of changes introduced
at the various stages of transmission.

However, it does seem possible to argue negatively: the spelling that appears in the Amherst Revelations is distinctly not
that of the 14th-century Norwich Guild Records, and seems to be
closer to that of the York Harrowing of Hell.[27] The argument
here is based on a limited number of isoglosses, whose selection
is necessarily arbitrary. Yet the evidence seems consistent
enough to place the language of the Amherst Revelations consi-
derably to the north of Norfolk, corroborating the morphological and phonological data:

Norwich Guilds	Amherst Revelations	York Harrowing
soule	sawle/saule	saule
owen	awne	awne
yeue	gyffe	giffe
shulle	schalle	schall
eueriche	ilke	ilke
her	thare	thare
-it (3 sg pres ind)	-es/-ys	-es/ys

To continue the negative argument: Davis (1954:119-44) includes
a number of dialectal criteria in his study of the 15th-century

26   Davis (1954:127) reports that the youngest John Paston nearly
     always spells 'like' as lyek.

27   Sisam (1967:171-84).

Norfolk dialect of the Pastons. He points out that, as there
is "a great variety of usage" among the Pastons themselves, it
is difficult to isolate a single characteristic as peculiar to
Norfolk. But the feature that is most pronounced (though not
invariable) is substitution of e for i (as heder, theder, wrete,
indeferent, parteculer, sperituall). The Guild Records exhibit
this trait (worschepe, yhef [='if']), as does Margery Kempe's
Book (wetyn, swech, whech). In contrast, although the Amherst
Revelations has a few forms in e (as whethyr [='whither'] and
trekylle [='trickle']), they are unusual: while the infrequency
of lowered i does not point anywhere else, it does seem to
point away from the Norfolk region.

c) Conclusion

The South, South East Midlands, and West Midlands are easily
excluded as possible locations for the dialect found in the
Amherst Revelations. The problem that emerges, then, is how
to evaluate the mixed northern and East Midland features, and,
at the same time, ascertain what the stages of transmission
have been. As Samuels asks (1969:327), "how does one establish
that a text is not written in a consistent dialect, but contains two or more strata"?

The weight of the evidence has consistently favoured the North.
The possibility that Julian or her amanuensis was northern cannot be excluded absolutely; but that she was from the Norfolk
region is certainly more likely (there are no northern features,
for instance, in any of the MSS of the longer version). Since
the language of the Amherst Revelations is distinctly not that
of Norfolk, the original language of the account must have been
altered, but altered by a scribe who was not consistently scrupulous in his transformation of the dialect: while a competent
scribe could usually be counted on to "make a very thorough job
of [a translation]...there are other cases where a scribe half-
transforms his original, producing a sort of Mischsprache"
(McIntosh 1963:8).

Thus we find, on the one hand, that the forms of the verb 'to
be' peculiar to Norfolk have been eliminated, and this conforms
to Forsström's point that "the forms of the verb 'to be'...

were especially apt to be translated" by Middle English scribes
(1948:9). On the other hand, relict forms, such as gostelye
and beholde, or the few characteristic Norfolk spellings (those
with lowered i, perhaps those with -ye-) can still be found.
There is a final aspect to the problem: the dialect recorded
in the Amherst Revelations is apparently not that of the Amherst scribe. Whoever made the Amherst MS is cousin to the
B.L. MS Harley 2409 scribe described by McIntosh (1963:9),
who reproduces each text in its own "self-consistent dialect".
As the following table shows, the Amherst scribe has laboured
to preserve the dialect of each of his exemplars.

	OE ā	Present participle	ch/k
Misyn translations[28]	gostelye holy knawen saule	knawande takande wyrkande	kyrke mykille sekyr slyke whilke
Goldyn pystille	awne gostely tone...toþer	euerlastynge stynkynge	mykylle suche whiche
Julian	anly awe gastelye haly knawe mare sawle/ saule tane...tothere	desyrande enioyande lenande schewande	kyrke mykille sekere swilke whilke
Ruysbroeck translation	holy knowe soule tone...toþere	abowndynge growynge indrawynge	chyrche iche syche whiche
Rolle	anely haly knawe mare nathynge saule swa waa	brennande spryngande	ilkane swylke whilke
Horologium sapientiae	gostely sawlle	euerlastande	mekille whilke
Myrroure of symple saules	gostely/ gastely holigoste knawe mare noon ooned soule/ saule	acordynge crauynge forgyffynge translatynge	chirche miche syche whiche

28   See pages 10, 12 for folio numbers. Examples recorded in this table
     are not always invariable, but they reflect the forms that appear

In sum, the mixed nature of the language of the Amherst Revelations, and the fact that this language is not that of the Amherst scribe himself, suggest at least two stages of transmission: Julian's Norwich manuscript; A's exemplar, dated by the incipit as 1413; and the Amherst MS itself, copied some time shortly after 1435. There may have been other steps involved, but there is no evidence to indicate that the 1413 exemplar was not itself the partially northernized version of Julian's original text.

4 The Corrector

As a whole, the Amherst MS has not been systematically corrected. In the Fyre of lufe, for example, which occupies 75 folios, there are twelve corrections, which involve restoring omitted words (as f.55v "that byrnynge of [lufe] vise & syns purgis", f.75v "and [als] truly") or repairing minor errors (at f.29v vnhede is altered to read onehede, at f.76v I is replaced by in). At f.68v an apparent instance of homoeoteleuton is repaired, but otherwise there is no evidence that the corrector made reference to another text. Other entries in the MS show even less sign of correction.

In striking contrast, the Revelations has been thoroughly corrected by a distinct scribe, C (whose hand, however, is several times found elsewhere in the MS, suggesting that he read it through). C's hand is roughly contemporary with A, and his language, too, seems to correspond with that of the Amherst Revelations. C has OE ā: mare (65/9); sch: schewed (46/5), lordeschyp (62/11); unvoicing of v: safe (40/15), hafe (51/30 luff (65/9). Whether C was working from a northern text, was himself from the North, or was simply adapting his additions to fit the language of the text, seems impossible to determine.

An interesting feature of many of C's corrections is that they correspond to the longer version, as in cases where A has made an obvious error or omission that disturbs the sense of the

regularly in each entry. Other striking discrepancies are gude in the Misyn translations and the Golden pystille vs. goode in Julian and Ruysbroeck; bun ('bound') in Misyn vs. bande in Rolle.

passage (see 42/22, 44/13, 46/13, 52/15). More striking, C has
noticed and repaired four instances of homoeoteleuton, one of
which (61/6) would not appear to be an omission unless A were
directly compared with another MS. Of the four, only one (50/
1) fails to match the reading of the longer version. In several instances, C "emends" A where there is no error, to produce
a reading that matches the longer version:

Amherst Revelations	[Corrector]/longer version
41/18 I wolde lyeve	I [hadd] lyeve
43/28 anly lovynge	[hamly] lovynge
44/26 oure god	[hyr] god
45/26 I saye	I [saw]

Elsewhere, C exhibits the unfortunate habit of erasing several
letters in a word and writing over them, rendering A's original
reading illegible. We cannot tell how, or why, C has altered
the text, but in most cases C's new readings again agree with
the longer version. Examples (where square brackets mark C's
changes) are: [if] 47/33, tha[i] 53/15, de[de] 53/19, rud[dy]
53/25, [of alle] 55/17, [saw] 56/1. These kinds of changes
reveal that C was not working from the same MS used by A, and
admit the possibility that the Amherst text may have been corrected from a copy of the longer version of the Revelations.

On the other hand, A contains a number of problematic readings
that have not been altered to accord with the longer version.
For example, at 43/17 A ends a sentence with "wrecchyd fleschly", while the reading in the longer version, almost certainly
correct, is "wretched flesh". Later, at 44/27-30, A reads

> that he wolde be borne of hir that was a sympille
> creature of his makynge. For this was hir merve-
> lynge that he that was hir makere walde be borne
> of hir that was a sympille creature of his makynge.

A's dittography does not appear in the longer version: P con-
cludes, "...he that was her maker would be borne of her that
was made". Again, A's obscure "ioye suffyrde hir felyd I..."
(54/32) could easily have been clarified had C referred to the
longer version: "...ioy suffer? Here felt I...". While the
longer version, as we know it, supplies the answers to each of
these difficult readings, C has failed to take advantage of
them.

In other cases, too, C seems ignorant of the longer text. A class of errors is found in A which, as they are based on homophones, may originally have resulted from dictation: A reads houre (50/19) where or is needed; A reads knawynge (61/19), man (64/19), foure (67/16), where reference to the longer version reveals that the correct readings must be knawyn, meen, for. But in these readings A stands uncorrected.

Further, if not final, evidence against correction from the longer version is C's introduction of gratuitous 'corrections' where A originally coincided with the longer version. Perhaps he saw them as improvements; possibly they were in the text he used; certainly, as they are otiose, they undermine his authority:

Amherst/ [Corrector]	longer version
40/25 [in] threttye ʒeere eelde	xxxth yeare olde
51/15 I see [I see]	I see
62/29 se [þat] thy selfe	se thy selfe

In sum, C does not emerge as a dependable witness; in a number of cases his alterations of A result in a manifestly inferior reading. Thus, in this edition, I admit his corrections only when A has been rendered illegible, or is corrupt.[29]

5 Differences Between the Short and the Longer Versions

The first editor of the Amherst Revelations, the Reverend Dundas Harford, advanced the theory that the short text "is what might be called the 'first edition' of the Revelations, and the longer form is the final outcome of twenty years' subsequent meditation, thought, and experience".[30] While there is no external evidence to prove that the short text is not, in fact, a later abridgement of the longer version, the discrepancies between the two versions support Harford's thesis that Amherst contains Julian's first responses. Further, Reynolds

---

29 As at 40/15, 41/21, 44/13, 46/5, 54/30, or the instances of homoeoteleuton: 50/1, 61/6-7, 62/11-2, 65/9.

30 Harford (1911:8); his theory is now generally accepted. See Molinari (1958:5), who, in his note, cites Thouless (1924:25), Underhill (no date:129), Coleman (1938:132), Renaudin (1945:63), and Hudleston (1952:xi), in support of Harford; see also Lawlor (1951:255-8).

(1956:xviii) points to the heading of Chapter 86 of the Sloane
MSS, which reads very like an apologia for a second edition:
"The Good lord shewid this book shuld be otherwise performid
than at the first writing".

A notable difference between the short text, A, and the longer
version, PSS, is the modification of personal references.
Throughout PSS the words I and me are frequently deleted; also
omitted are such phrases as me thought that (43/9), & my desyre (46/29), as he dyd to me (46/31), as it es to me (49/1).
Such changes are presumably attributable to Julian's later
belief, in keeping with her particular modesty, that she had
first made the account too intimate, too much her own.

Some personal passages in A are excluded entirely or severely
abridged in PSS. The incident in which Julian's mother, thinking her dead, closes her eyes (54/19-23), is deleted, as is her
disclaimer about being a woman "leued febille & freylle" (47/
34-48/14). Her reference to the story of St. Cecilia which
she "harde a man telle of halye kyrke" (40/26), and the sug-
gestion of her identification with that saint, are omitted.
Alteration of A's phrase "atte my bedde feete" (72/12) to read
"before my face" dispels the image of Julian lying in her sick
bed. In the short text, when Julian falls ill, the curate
comes to her bedside, and brings with him a child and a cross
(41/29ff.); he calls her "Dow3tter"; her hands fall, her head
settles "on syde", her friends prop up her head with cloths:
in the longer version these details, which lend such immediacy
to the account, are rendered less personal, or omitted al-
together.

The modification of personal references may be seen as part of
a general effort to improve the text; this same kind of editorial impulse is reflected in the alteration, also noted by Windeatt,[31] of the passage about the Virgin and the hazel nut in
the first Revelation. While in A the image of the hazel nut

---

31 (1977:7-8): he describes the revision as "a literary improvement of
    a badly organized passage", but goes on to add that "the awkwardness
    of the A order indeed represents that of life".

occurs both before and after the sight of "oure ladye", PSS has
been neatened so that the vision of the Virgin comes first, the
hazel nut follows. Possibly the revised sequence in PSS is
based on Julian's own recapitulation of the revelation (45/
28ff.), and certainly the effect is to make the account seem
more logical. But the sense of immediacy is lost: the nature
of the shewing is that Julian sees many things at once, and
each contributes to the understanding of the others. The apparent confusion in A, the result of Julian's attempt to describe all aspects of the experience simultaneously, reflects
her excitement and her concern to record the shewing while her
memory is fresh.

In other ways, too, A's sense of urgency is qualified: PSS in-
troduce conventional, pious phrases that have the air of be-
lated amplifications:

	A	PSS
40/29	by the styrrynge of this	by the grace of god and teaching of holie church
42/4	to come	to come by the mercie of god
47/31	I am sekere	I hope by the grace of god
74/1	in pees	in pease by hys grace

But on the other hand, much of the additional material in the
longer version brings great richness to Julian's account, and,
as Windeatt points out (1977:7), "sets the shewings within a
wider frame of reference". Her description of the crucifixion,
for example, is greatly expanded.[32] Other striking images
help to illuminate her point: the sea bed, the Harrowing of
Hell, the moribund body and the child's spirit; and fuller
explanations serve to clarify the meaning of the shewings as
it has been revealed to her in the intervening years.[33]

Elsewhere, changes in PSS seem aimed at correcting theolog-
ically unsound impressions. While Julian's first version im-
plies that only contemplatives are eligible for the mystical
experience (45/9ff.), PSS omit these passages: similarly,

32 See Notes to 45/24, 49/19, 50/8-9, 53/27, 54/11.
33 See Notes to 49/23, 50/19, 56/27, 57/31, 61/7, 71/2.

Hilton's _Mixed_ _Life_ and the _Abbey_ _of_ _the_ _Holy_ _Ghost_ furnish
evidence of the growing belief in the 14th and 15th centuries
that union was not reserved for solitaries.[34]

A notes that "in manne ys god & so in man ys alle" (47/23-4);
P substitutes "and in god is alle" for the second half of the
phrase, while SS read "& God is in alle": the _Book_ warns of
the Pantheistic heresy, "[God] is þi being & þou not his"
(Hodgson 1958:lvii,136).

Julian's "ylke man" (53/1) is modified in PSS to read "some
soules": the extreme trials endured by Julian are not required
for the soul to be close to God and know his love. Her remark
that she would like to have "dyede bodylye" (55/1), suggesting
an active longing for death, is replaced in PSS by one which
simply expresses her deep sorrow at seeing Christ in pain.

Between the first and second "editions" of the _Revelations_,
then, the emphasis shifts from the experience towards its sig-
nificance and what Windeatt calls "a more universalist posi-
tion" (1977:3). Personal details are omitted, a sense of immediacy is lost; on the other hand a great body of descriptive
and explanatory material enriches the narrative. And, as Shepherd says, although she has "turned her illuminations over and
over...she never transcends her purpose of recording her initial experiences".[35]

6 The _Relationship_ _of_ _the_ _MSS_

The relationship between the Amherst text and the three MSS of
the longer version is not entirely clear.[36] Most of the differences lie between A and PSS, which is hardly surprising:
as discussed in section 5, the longer version amounts to a
second edition of the _Revelations_, and presumably most of these
alterations are attributable to Julian herself.

---

34   Horstmann (1895:I,264,321).

35   Shepherd (1970:74).

36   For example, in the first 7 folios of A, A disagrees with PSS 186
     times; AP stand against SS 78 times, while ASS stand against P 33
     times; APS1 stand against S2 52 times, and AS1 against PS2 7 times.

P often supports A against SS, and these cases, where the AP
reading is almost certainly Julian's, suggest that SS share a
later revision. A few examples follow:

	AP	SS
39/11	to haue	om
40/2-3	this was my menynge for I wolde aftyr becawse of that schewynge	the cause of this peti-tion was that after the sheweing I should
42/28	gyfte	gracious gift
46/14	and gafe me space & tyme	with time & space
49/26-7	syght...syght	sight

But elsewhere, P too shows clear evidence of having undergone
a separate revision, by a scribe with distinctive habits. For
example:

	ASS	P
40/10	dye	haue died
40/21	have	might haue
41/25	styrrede	holpen
44/16	aned	vnyted
56/17	noghthede	condempnyd

Generally, P exhibits a conscious preference for auxiliary
verbs and "modern" equivalents; occasionally the concurrence
of ASS seems to reveal an unintentional error on P's part
(or that of his original), as:

	ASS	P
59/37	forseande (forseyng S1 allforeseeing S2)	forseyde
63/5	anynge	comyng
77/30	waykenesse	wyckydnesse

The Sloane MSS, then, as has just been seen, often support A
against P; and they also appear to have undergone their own
distinct evolution. In addition, the frequent agreement of APS1
against S2 reveals that the later S2 was itself revised, by a
scribe with a tendency even more marked than that found in P to
substitute "modern" synonyms:

	APS1	S2
41/7	wenyd	thought
42/22	kynde	nature

	APS1	S2
43/9	garlonde	crown
43/22	of fendys	by the devils

There are points at which all four MSS disagree, where the vari-
ants could have been introduced at unknown stages in the course
of transmission, or could represent the tinkering of the actual
scribes who made P, S1, S2, or for that matter, A. A few examples follow:

39/24-5   were belevande his paynes that tyme and sythene] A,
           were lyuyng that tyme and saw his paynes P,
           seene that time his peynes S1,
           at that time saw his paines S2

40/9   take] A, vndertaken P, vnderfongyn S1, receive S2

43/2   ne (2)] A, no P, <u>om</u> S1, any S2

45/1   sawe sothfastlye] A, did vnderstande verily P,
           understoode sothly S1, understood truly S2

Elsewhere, P and SS disagree with each other, and with A. It is
not always obvious which of the three reflects Julian's own readings: A could be the original, with either P or SS representing
Julian's revision, or the A reading could itself reflect a later
alteration:

	A	P	SS
39/6	thre graces be the gyfte	before thre gyftes by the grace	afore iij gifts
39/10	grete	sumdeele	sume
39/26	suffrede	haue suffered	suffer
39/27	atte	when	<u>om</u>
42/24	that I schulde lyeve	to haue liued	to levyn

Thus the MSS of the longer version divide into two families,
P on the one hand, SS on the other.[37] Both branches appear to
have undergone their own separate revision subsequent to Julian's second edition; additionally, S2 has been "modernized" by

37   There are several points in the text where S1 supports A against PS2,
     but in these cases the PS2 reading can be attributed to coincidence.
     All are common substitutions, and each, in addition, reflects the ten-
     dency shown individually by P and S2 to provide "modern" equivalents, as:
         40/21   woote] AS1, knowest PS2
         43/22   or] AS1, before PS2
         55/4   mykillehede] AS1, grettnes PS2

a later scribe; and related to, or descended from, P are Upholland, Westminster, and the Cressy text. If this much information is then combined with the conclusions about the Amherst
text, it is possible to propose a stemma which, if not complete,
seems to express the broad relationship between the known texts
of Julian's work: [38]

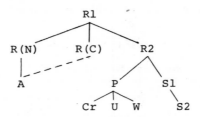

7 Julian's Subject Matter

At the end of the first Revelation (48/21-3) Julian tells us
that

> Alle this blyssede techynge of oure lorde god was schewyd
> to me in thre partyes, that is be bodylye syght, and be
> worde formede in myne vndyrstandynge, & be gastelye syght.

Molinari (1958:36,41) equates the bodily sights with those shewings that include "a corporeal object--mainly the Humanity of
Christ", and describes the ghostly visions as "exclusively con-
cerned with purely spiritual objects".

Some of the shewings fall squarely into one or the other of
these categories.[39] In Revelations ii, iv, viii, and x, Julian
sees images of the crucified Christ; she speaks of seeing "with
bodely syght the face of the crucifixe" (49/14), of "behaldande
the bodye plentevouslye bledande" (50/7). These four shewings
seem without question to fall into the first of Julian's "thre
partyes".

---

38 R1=Julian's first version   Cr=Cressy
    R(N)=Northernized version of R1   U=Upholland
    R(C)=Hypothetical copy used by C   W=Westminster
    R2=Julian's second edition

39 See Molinari (1958:60ff.) for a comparison between Julian's classi-
    fication of her shewings and the 'classical' scheme (corporeal, ima-
    ginative, intellectual); also St. Augustine, De Genesi ad litteram,
    PL, 34,458ff.; Contra Adimantum, PL, 42,171.

Likewise, certain of the shewings seem to be distinctly "gastelye": in Revelation iii she sees God "in a poynte, that es in
myne vndyrstandynge" (49/24); in Revelation vi she is shown the
three degrees of bliss reserved for those who have wilfully
served God; and in Revelation vii she is shown a "souerayne
gastelye lykynge in my sawlle" (52/12-3).[40]

It is possible for a shewing to contain both bodily and ghostly
aspects. In Revelation i, as Molinari points out,[41] Julian
first sees "the rede blode trekylle downe fro vndyr the garlande" (43/7), and this sight continues throughout the entire
shewing; but, in addition, "this same tyme that I sawe this bodyly syght, oure lorde schewyd me a gastelye sight of his anly lovynge" (43/27). Later when "god brought owre ladye to myne vndyrstandynge", Julian sees her "gastelye in bodilye lyekenes"
(44/22): the two aspects, bodily and ghostly, cooperate to reveal God as "the makere, the lovere, the kepere" (44/15).

What then of the "worde formede", Julian's second "partye"?
The words are, for the most part, spoken by Christ to Julian,
and reflect the special closeness between them as he explains,
guides, and comforts her during the shewings. In Revelation v,
God gives her time to "behalde langere" all that she has seen:

> than was withowtyn voyce & withowte openynge of lyppes
> formede in my sawlle this worde, "Herewith ys the feende
> ouercomyn". This worde sayde oure lorde menande his
> passyon (50/21-4).

40 To facilitate reference, I provide a table of the correspondences
    between chapters, revelations, and pages.

I	39	iv	50/7	XIII	58	XIX	67
II	41	v	50/19	x	58/23	xiv	67/16
III	42	IX	51	xi	58/30	XX	70
i	43/7	vi	51/23	xii	59/18	xv	70/7
IV	43	vii	52/12	xiii	59/32	XXI	72
V	45	x	53	XIV	61	XXII	73
VI	46	viii	53/17	XV	62	xvi	73/15
VII	48	XI	56	XVI	64	XXIII	74
VIII	49	XII	56	XVII	65	XXIV	77
ii	49/14	ix	56/28	XVIII	66	XXV	78
iii	49/24						

41 (1958:48); Molinari argues that between the ghostly and the bodily
    lies another, intermediate type of shewing that itself consists of
    two parts, "ghostly sight in bodily likeness", and "more ghostly
    sight without bodily likeness".

And through these words she is led to the second, ghostly phase
of the shewing, wherein she perceives the "vnmyght" of the
fiend.

Similarly, Revelation ix opens with Christ's question, "'Arte
thou wele payde that I suffyrde for the?'" (56/28). The subsequent dialogue between Julian and Christ leads to the ghostly
stage, wherein her "vndyrstandynge was lyftyd vppe into heuen,
and thare I sawe thre hevens" (57/4). Revelation x combines the
bodily type and the "worde formede"; Christ looks into his open
side and says, "'Loo, how I lovyd the'". This short and simple
shewing serves as a break from the exalted complexity of the
preceding one,

> as ȝyf he hadde sayde: My childe, ȝyf thow kan nought loke
> in my godhede, see heere howe I lette opyn my syde, and
> my herte be clovene in twa (58/24-7).

In each of the final six shewings, which are essentially ghostly
Christ speaks directly to Julian. For example, in Revelation xi
Julian is shown the "gastelye syght of [oure ladye]...hye and
nobille and gloriouse and plesaunte" (59/4-6); but first, Christ
looks down from the cross and says to Julian, "'Wille thowe see
hir?'" (58/32). In Revelation xii, Julian sees "oure lorde...
mare gloryfyed...than I sawe hym before" (59/18), yet "eftyr thi
techynge" Christ speaks to her in the same direct, familiar tone
"hamelye, curtayse and blysfulle and verray lyfe" (59/22).

The words reveal that Julian is loved, and also that her "evyn-
cristen" are safe: in Revelation xiii she is shown the extreme-
ly complex nature of sin and its relation to the passion; the
difficult and frightening aspect of the lesson is "redely passed
ouere ... for oure goode lorde god walde noght that the saule
ware afferdede of this vglye syght" (60/23-5), and then to
soften it, Christ reassures her directly, "'Synne is behouelye'" (60/11), "'alle schalle be wele, and alle maner of thynge
schalle be wele'" (60/33). Again, as the operation of prayer
is revealed in Revelation xiv, he offers her words of comfort:
"'I am grownde of thy besekynge'", he explains, "'howe schulde
it than be that þou schulde nought hafe thy besekynge?'" (68/
7,10-1).

Responding to her desire to be delivered from this world, God explains in Revelation xv that soon enough she will be taken from her pain: "'Whate schulde it than greve the to suffyr a-while, sen it is my wille and my wirschippe?'" (70/22-3). And finally, after the glorious vision of the soul as kingdom with Christ sitting in its midst, in Revelation xvi, he turns to her, as it seems, and says, "'Witte it welle, it was na rauynge that thowe sawe today'" (74/9-10). It is almost as if he is at her bedside, and they are experiencing the shewing together.

However the "worde formede" may fit into a technical scheme, it is clear that they are crucial to establishing and sustaining the relationship of intimate affection between Julian and her Lord. His special tenderness balances the awesome aspect of the revelations, and reassures her of his love through the most trying and painful times. What surprises her is not God's splendour, but his humanity:

> I was astonnyd for wondere & merveyle that y had that
> he wolde be so hamelye with a synfulle creature (43/15-6).

Christ's homeliness, and his desire for oneness with the soul, are the most convincing proof of his love,

> He es oure clethynge, for loove wappes vs and wyndes
> vs, halses vs and alle beseches vs, hynges aboute vs
> for tendyr loove, that he maye nevere leve vs (43/30-2),

and Julian's perception of this homeliness is the basis for the "comfortabylle wordes" (39/4) that she offers to Christ's lovers. She makes it her goal in the Revelations to pass on her confidence to those who may themselves be troubled by doubt:

> ...in alle this I was mekylle styrrede in charyte to myne
> evyncrystene that thaye myght alle see and knawe þe same
> that I sawe, for I walde that it ware comforthe to thame
> alle as it es to me (48/30-49/1).

For unlike The Cloud of Unknowing and The Scale of Perfection, Julian's work is not a guide book for solitaries; and she gives no attention to the question of right ascetic preparation for the contemplative life. Her words are for "alle thaye that de-syres to be crystes looveres" (39/5).

Thus Julian stresses the universal aspect of her shewings. They are "generalle & nathynge in specyalle" (49/2, 64/32-3); "comon & generale as we ar alle ane" (47/6-7). And they are not to be

seen as a special sign of God's favour: when Julian asks for
news of a particular friend, she is refused the information:

> 'Take it generally...for it is mare worschippe to god to
> behalde hym in alle than in any specyalle thynge' (64/20-2).

But despite the universal aim of the Revelations, the context
is autobiographical, and the work derives great strength from
this fact. There is nothing theoretical about her account, and
its realism gives it a remarkable authenticity. She smells the
smoke of the fiend and cries, "'Is alle on fyre that is here?'"
(73/5); she feels such "hevynes and werynesse of myselfe...that
vnnethes I cowthe hafe pacyence to lyeve" (52/18-20); she is
"sare aschamed for my reklessenes" (72/15); and she jokes with
herself to ease her fear after her second struggle with the
fiend, "...'walde þou nowe fra this tyme euermare be so besy to
kepe the fro synne, this ware a soferayne & a goode occupacion'"
(75/17-8).

Concrete descriptions, as those of her own physical illness,
are notable for their precision:

> Aftyr this my syght byganne to fayle and it was alle
> dyrke abowte me in the chaumbyr...the overe partye of
> my bodye beganne to dye as to my felynge. Myne handdys
> felle downe on aythere syde, and also for vnpowere my
> heede satylde downe on syde...(42/8ff.).

Julian is scrupulous in reporting each detail of her shewings,
though sometimes at the expense of conciseness:

> I sawe that swete faace as yt ware drye and bludyelesse
> with pale dyinge, sithen mare dede pale langourande; and
> than turnede more dede to the blewe & sithene mare blewe
> as the flesche turnede mare deepe dede...and namelye in
> the lyppes. Thare I sawe this foure colourse, thaye that
> I sawe beforehande freschlye & ruddy, lyflye & lykande to
> my syght...also the nese claungede and dryed to my sight
> (53/18ff.).

But while accuracy is a prime obligation, it does not forbid
the inclusion of formal, rhythmic passages that heighten the
devotional effect of the prose:

> ...luffe was withowtyn begynnynge & es and evere schalle
> be withowtyn any ende (56/20-2);

> ...nane is mare, nane is lesse, nane is hiare, nane is
> lawere, botte evene like in blysse (57/7-9);

> ...we ere his blysse, we er his mede, we er his wyr-
> schippe, we er his crowne (57/20-1).

These repetitive passages are woven into Julian's careful, factual account, and the two elements combine to make her testimony the more convincing: she communicates not only the specific details, but the sense of fervour to which they gave rise.

The Revelations opens with a description of three wishes, made by Julian in her youth:

> The fyrst was to have mynde of cryste es passion, the
> seconde was bodelye syekenes, and the thryd was to haue
> of goddys gyfte thre woundys (39/6-9) ...the wounde of
> contricyon, the wounde of compassyon, & the wounde of
> wylfulle langgynge to god (40/32-3).

The sickness, which seems to be an aspect of the "wounde of contricyon", comes in her thirty-first year. The priest brings a cross to her bedside, and she "sette myne eyen in the face of the crucyfixe" (42/5-6). Her sight fails and the room grows dark, but "in the ymage of the crosse there helde a comon lyght" (42/10-1).

It is difficult here to ignore the similarity between Julian's experience and the contemplative process as described in the Cloud: a naked intent unto God and forgetting of the self; a passive waiting in the dark night, an ordeal that acts as a purgatory; finally the perception of light through the darkness:

> ...a beme of goostly liȝt, peersyng þis cloude of vn-
> knowing þat is bitwix þee & hym, & schewe þee sum of
> his priuete...Þan schalt þou fele þine affeccion en-
> flaumid wiþ þe fiire of his loue (Hodgson 1958:62).

Walter Hilton also speaks of the soul's progress through night to light, in which the darkness is caused by desire for Jesus' love: "soothly the murkier that this night is, the nearer is the true day of the love of Jhesu" (Underhill 1948:321-2).

Julian's room grows dark, "the overe partye of my bodye beganne to dye" (42/14), and she believes herself to be at the point of death. "Sodeynlye", as she contemplates the crucifix, "alle my payne was awaye fro me and I was alle hole" (42/19-20); she recalls her wish for the second wound, compassion, "that he walde fulfylle my bodye with mynde of felynge of his blessede passyon" (42/28-9), and the first shewing begins.

Her compassion amounts to a kind of identification and answers her original desire to "have the more trewe mynde in the pas-

sion of cryste" (40/3-4). The three wounds match the wounds
of the suffering Christ; and as Julian contemplates his figure
they are united through the combined working of contrition,
compassion, and wilful longing:

> Here I sawe a grete anynge betwyx criste and vs, for
> when he was in payne, we ware in payne (55/10-1).

The oneness between Christ and the soul, as effected by the
passion and its contemplation, is revealed; also shown in the
course of the Revelations is the process whereby the soul, sep-
arated from God through sin, may regain the divine likeness,
and Julian's treatment here again recalls the Cloud. Before
Hilton's highest level of contemplation - a combination of
cognition and affection - can be achieved, the soul must be
reformed in God's image:

> But after great plenty of grace and mickle ghostly
> travail a soul may come thereto; and that is when he
> is first healed of his ghostly sickness...new gracious
> feelings are brought in with burning love and ghostly
> light. Then neareth a soul to perfection and to re-
> forming in feeling (1948:287).

Sin destroys God's likeness in the soul, Hilton says, but in
turn the "image of sin can be broken down in thee and destroyed,
by the which thou art forshapen from the kindly shape of the
image of Christ" (1948:219). Similarly, Julian remarks that
"þow3 the saule be euer lyke god in kynde and in substaunce,
it is oft vnlike in condicion thurgh syn of mannes party".
But when, as in prayer, "the sawlle wille as god wille...than
es it lyke to god in condicyon as it es in kynde" (68/26ff.)

Of sin itself, Hilton says

> Soothly it is nought....This nought is nought else but
> darkness of conscience, a lacking of love and of light
> ...sin is nought but a wanting of God (1847:127-8).

Julian, too, maintains that sin has no being in itself:

> Botte I sawe noght synne, fore I lefe it has na manere
> of substaunce, na partye of beynge (60/25-6).

Yet the pain that it causes can lead to good, "for it purges
vs and makes vs to knawe oureselfe and aske mercy" (60/28-9).[42]

---

42 Julian's discussion of sin as a positive force corresponds to the
    traditional idea of the "second conversion" described by Molinari
    (1958:78) as the "stage in which man...sees the disorder of his life,
    deliberately turns to God and begins to desire him ardently, per-
    ceiving that he alone can satisfy the soul's longing".

As the "scharpyste scourge" (65/29) it can lead the soul to contrition, and "as it es punysched here with sorowe and with pennaunce it schalle be rewarded in heuen" (66/15-6).

Prayer, for Julian, is necessary to join the soul to God, or,
to use Hilton's phrase, to reform it in God's image. She speaks
of two kinds of prayer, seeking and beholding, but they are part
of the same process.[43] The closer the soul gets to God, the
less active the seeking, but the seeking itself pleases God.
She describes the process in detail:

> "I am grownde of thy besekynge. First it is my wille
> that þou hafe it, & syne I make the to will it, & syne
> I make the to beseke it, & 3if þou beseke, howe schulde
> it than be that þou schulde nought hafe thy besekynge?"
> (68/7-11).
>
> ...he wille þat we be sekere to hafe oure prayere, for
> prayer pleses god....Praiere anes the saule to god....
> Than makes prayer þe saule like vnto god...he haldes
> vs parcyners of his goode deede (68/23ff.).

A forgetting of temporal concerns is essential:

> God wille be knawen, & hym lykes þat we reste vs in hym
> ....When [the saule] is noughthid for love to hafe hym
> that is alle that is goode, than es he abylle to resayue
> gostlye reste (45/19ff.);

and the soul must strive to subject itself to God: "Bot he be
boxom, na maner of prayer makes god souple to hym" (69/22-3).
Here the reciprocal nature of the process is most clear. In
a state of union the soul and God are in perfect accord, each
obeys the other, their wills converge, their love is mutual:

> "I am gladde that þou erte comen to reste, for I hafe
> euer loved the & nowe loves the, and þou me" (70/2-4).

The theme of reciprocal love recalls the initial step in the
joining of the soul to God - the working of compassion - which
gave rise to Julian's first shewing; it also reflects the more
general identification between Julian and her Lord throughout
the revelations:

> ...howe myght my payne be more than to see hym that
> es alle my lyfe, alle my blys, & alle mye ioye suf-
> fyr? (54/30-2).

43 "Whate tyme that mannes saule es hamelye with god, hym nedes nought to
    praye, botte behalde reuerentlye" (69/13-4): by "praye" Julian here
    means "beseke"; "behalde" refers to the higher level of prayer. Cf.
    Molinari's discussion of Julian's treatment of prayer (1958:94-139).

Her pain at Christ's suffering could not be more profound. Yet
as the process of redemption is revealed to Julian, the central
image of the crucified Christ becomes a joyful one. Each of
the bodily sights, no matter how painful, leads to a greater
affirmation of God's infinite love and strength. Julian,
though she has just seen the "bodye plentevouslye bledande"
(50/7), can be jubilant at the impotence of the fiend: "For
this syght I lugh3 myghttelye" (51/7-8); as she contemplates
the face of the dying Christ, his expression becomes blissful,
and she is "alle gladde & mery as yt was possybille":

> Than brought oure lorde merelye to my mynde, "Whate
> es any poynte of thy payne or of þy grefe?" And I
> was fulle merye (56/25-7).

In Julian's final vision the image of the loving and the power-
ful God are fused, she sees him,

> verraye god & verray man, a fayre persone and of large
> stature, wyrschipfulle hiest lorde...cledde solemplye
> in wyrschippes (73/20-2),

seated in the kingdom of the soul, where he "rewles & 3emez
heuen & erth and alle that is" (73/23-4). Yet despite his glorious omnipotence,

> The place that Ihesu takes in oure saule he schalle
> neuer remove it withowtyn ende, for in vs is his
> haymelyeste hame & maste lykynge to hym to dwelle
> in (73/28-30).

8 Editorial Method

Capitalization, word-division, and punctuation are editorial;
quotation marks are reserved for words as they are actually
spoken or first heard by Julian. MS spelling has been retained,
except that j is transcribed as i. The major textual divisions
found in A have been followed, and are indicated by large Roman
numerals, but paragraph divisions are editorial. Small Roman
numerals in the left hand margin mark the beginning of each
shewing. Abbreviations are expanded silently, to conform with
scribal orthography. It is not always easy to distinguish between abbreviations and meaningless flourishes, as the scribe
himself is inconsistent, but I have tried to rely on the forms
spelled out by A in the text as the basis for expansion: thus
-r' and -ł are given as -re and -le, -c̄oñ as -cyon, and āñ- as

aun-. On the other hand, though -o̅n often occurs, as in passion
or reson, I have not expanded, since the superior mark may indicate -oun, -one (cf. passyone 73/20, resone 41/21), or
nothing at all.

Emendations - both mine and C's - are marked by square brackets;
editorial omissions are indicated by [+]. C's corrections, when
they have not been admitted, are recorded in the textual appara-
tus at the bottom of the page. Emendations are adapted to scribal orthography, and the readings of APSS provided in the appa-
ratus. Amongst the MSS of the longer version I assume a hierarchy: if the variant reflects the reading of PSS, I follow P's
spelling, if that of S1 and S2, I follow S1. When an emendation
requires explanation, it is provided in the Notes, which begin
on page 80.

As the Amherst text is at least two steps removed from the
archetype - one of these steps involving translation of dialect
- it is not possible to reconstruct the original version. None-
theless, when A appears to be corrupt, I have tried to recover
Julian's intended reading, and in this effort have been assis-
ted by reference to the MSS of the longer version. In cases
where A has apparently omitted small words or single letters
(as final -s or -d), PSS confirm that the reading suggested by
common sense is in fact correct (as 40/16, 40/32, 41/1, 41/15,
47/6). Similarly, in cases of incorrect word division (as
54/25, 56/13), haplography (69/2), dittography (58/24), or
minim confusion (50/23), PSS verify the corrections that sense
dictates. Elsewhere, where A's corruption and its repair may
be less than obvious, reference to PSS can reveal the origin
of the error and how it may be corrected (as 40/24, 42/22,
44/30, 45/14-5, 50/19). However far PSS may be from their
archetype, they have proved valuable witnesses in producing a
text that, it is hoped, reflects Julian's original intention
as nearly as possible.

REVELATIONS OF DIVINE LOVE

I

There es a vision schewed be the goodenes of god to a deuoute
woman and hir name es Iulyan that is recluse atte Norwyche and
ȝitt ys on lyfe anno domini millesimo CCCCxiii, in the whilke
visyon er fulle many comfortabylle wordes and gretly styrrande
to alle thaye that desyres to be crystes looverse.

I desyrede thre graces be the gyfte of god. The fyrst was
to have mynde of cryste es passion, the seconde was bodelye
syekenes, and the thryd was to haue of goddys gyfte thre woundys. For the fyrste come to my mynde with devocyon: me thought
I hadde grete felynge in the passyon of cryste, botte ȝitte I
desyrede to haue mare be the grace of god. Me thought I wolde
haue bene that tyme with Mary Mawdeleyne and with othere that
were crystes loverse, that I myght have sene bodylye the passion of oure lorde that he sufferede for me, that I myght have
sufferede with hym as othere dyd that lovyd hym. Notwithstandynge that, I leevyd sadlye alle the peynes of cryste as halye
kyrke schewys & techys, & also the payntyngys of crucyfexes
that er made be the grace of god aftere the techynge of haly
kyrke to the lyknes of crystes passyon als farfurthe as man ys
witte maye reche.

Nouȝtwithstondynge alle this trewe beleve, I desyrede a bodylye syght whareyn y myght have more knawynge of bodelye paynes
of oure lorde oure savyoure, and of the compassyon of oure ladye and of alle his trewe loverse that were belevande his paynes that tyme and sythene; for I wolde have beene one of thame
and suffrede with thame. Othere syght of gode ne schewynge
desyrede I nevere none tylle atte the sawlle were departyd

6   Unexplained capital S precedes I.

frome the bodye, for I trayste sothfastlye that I schulde be
safe, and this was my menynge; for I wolde aftyr, becawse of
that schewynge, have the more trewe mynde in the passion of
cryste.

5   For the seconde, come to my mynde with contricion, frelye withowtyn any sekynge, a wylfulle desyre to hafe of goddys gyfte a
bodelye syekenes. And I wolde þat this bodylye syekenes myght
have beene so harde as to the dede, [f.97v] so that I myght in
the sekenes take alle my ryghtynges of halye kyrke, wenande
10 myselfe that I schulde dye; and that alle creatures that sawe
me myght wene the same, for I wolde hafe no comforth of no
fleschlye nothere erthelye lyfe. In this sekenes I desyrede
to hafe alle manere of paynes bodelye & gastelye that I schulde
have 3yf I schulde dye, alle the dredes & tempestes of feyndys
15 & alle manere of [othere] paynes [safe] of the ow3te passynge
of the sawlle, for I hope[d] that it my3t be to me a spede when
I schulde dye, for I desyrede sone to be with my god.

This two desyres of the passyon and of the seekenes I desyrede
thame with a condicyon, for me thought that it passede the com-
20 ene course of prayers. And therfore I sayde, "Lorde, thowe
woote whate I wolde. 3yf it be thy wille that I have itt,
grawnte itt me. And 3yf it be nou3t thy wille, goode lorde,
be nought dysplesede, for I wille nought botte as thowe wille".
This sekenes desyrede I yn my [3]ought þat y myght have it
25 whene I were threttye 3eere eelde.

For the thirde, I harde a man telle of halye kyrke of the
storye of <u>Saynte Cecylle</u>, in the whilke schewynge I vndyrstode
that sche hadde thre woundys with a swerde in the nekke, with
the whilke sche pynede to the dede. By the styrrynge of this
30 I conseyvede a myghty desyre, prayande oure lorde god that he
wolde grawnte me thre woundys in my lyfe tyme, that es to saye
the wound[e] of contricyon, the wounde of compassyon, [&] the
wounde of wylfulle langgynge to god. Ryght as I askede the

15 othere] P, þayre A. <u>om</u> SS; safe] CP, except SS, <u>om</u> A. 16 hoped] CP,
hope A. 24 3ought] P, thought A. 25 <u>C</u> <u>inserts</u> in <u>before</u> <u>threttye</u>, <u>om</u>
PSS. 32 wounde] PSS, woundys A; &] CPSS, <u>om</u> A.

othere two with a condyscyon, [so] I askyd the thyrde withowtyn any condyscyon. This two desyres beforesayde passed
fro my mynde, and the thyrde dwellyd contynuelye.

II

Ande when I was thryttye wyntere alde and a halfe, god sente
me a bodelye syekenes in the whilke I laye thre dayes and thre
nyghttes, and on the ferthe nyght I toke alle my ryghttynges
of haly kyrke, and wenyd nought tylle haue lyffede tylle daye.
And aftyr this y langourede furthe two dayes & two nyghttes;
& on the thyrde nyght I wenede ofte tymes to hafe passede,
and so wenyd thaye that were abowte me. Botte in this I was
ryght sarye & lothe thou3t for to dye, botte for nothynge
that was [f.98r] in erthe that me lykede to lyeve fore, nor
for nothynge that I was aferde fore, for I tristyd in god.
Botte it was fore I walde hafe lyevede to have lovede god better and lange tyme, that [I] myght, be the grace of that lyevynge, have the more knowynge and lovynge of god in the blysse
of hevene.

For me thought alle the tyme that I wolde lyeve here so lytille and so schorte in the regarde of endeles blysse, I
thou3t thus, "Goode lorde, maye my lyevynge be no langere to
thy worschippe?" And [I] was aunswerde in my resone, and be
the felynges of my paynes, that I schulde dye. And I asentyd
fully with alle the wille of mye herte to be atte god ys wille.

Thus I endurede tille daye, and by than was my bodye dede fra
the myddys downwarde as to my felynge. Than was I styrrede
to [be] sette vppe ryghttes, lenande with clothes to my heede
for to have the mare fredome of my herte to be atte goddes
wille, and thynkynge on hym whilys my lyfe walde laste. And
thay.that were with me sente for the person my curette to be
atte myne endynge. He come, and a childe with hym, and brought
a crosse, & be thane I hadde sette myne eyen and myght nou3t
speke. The persone sette the crosse before my face and sayde,
"Dow3tter, I have brought the the ymage of thy sauioure. Loke

---

1 so] CP, om A. 15 I] PSS, om A. 18 C inserts hadd above wolde, which
is subpunged. 21 I] CPSS, om A. 26 be] CPSS, om A.

thereopon, & comforthe the þerewith, in reverence of hym that
dyede for the & me".

Me thou3t þan that y was welle, for myne eyen ware sette vp-
warde into heveñe whethyr I trustede for to come. Botte nevere-
5 thelesse I assendyd to sette myne eyen in the face of the crucyfixe 3if y myght, for to endure the langyr in to the tyme of
myn endynge; for m[e] thought I my3t langyr endure to loke evyn
forthe than vppe ryght. Aftyr this my syght byganne to fayle,
and it was alle dyrke abowte me in the chaumbyr, and myrke as
10 it hadde bene nyght; save in the ymage of the crosse there
helde a comon lyght, and I wyste nevere howe. Alle that was
besyde the crosse was huglye to me as 3yf it hadde bene mykylle
occupyede with fendys.

Aftyr this the overe partye of my bodye beganne to dye as to
15 my felynge. Myne handdys felle downe on aythere syde, and also
for vnpowere my heede satylde down [f.98v] on syde. The maste
payne that I felyd was schortnes of wynde and faylynge of lyfe.
Than wende I sothelye to hafe bene atte the poynte of dede.

And in this sodeynlye alle my payne was awaye fro me and I was
20 alle hole, and namelye in the overe partye of my bodye, as evere I was before or aftyr. I merveylede of this chaunge, for
me thought it was a [de]rne wyrkynge of god, & nought of kynde.
And 3itte be the felynge of this ese I trystede nevere the mare
that I schulde lyeve, ne the felynge of this ese was ne fulle
25 ese to me. For me thou3t I hadde leuere have bene delyverede
of this worlde, for my herte was wilfulle thereto.

III

And sodeynlye come vnto my mynde that I schulde desyre the seconde wounde of oure lordes gyfte and of his grace, that he walde fulfylle my bodye with mynde of felynge of his blessede pas-
30 syon, as I hadde before prayede. For I wolde that his paynes
ware my paynes, with compassyon, & aftyrwarde langynge to god.
Thus thou3t me that I myght, with his grace, have his woundys

---

7 me] CSS, my P, C adds -e over erasure. 22 derne] Iourne A, pryue CPS1,
secret S2, C adds pryue above line, Iourne struck out and subpunged.

that I hadde before desyrede. But in this I desyrede neuere
ne bodely syght, ne no manere schewynge of god, botte compassyon, as me thought that a kynde sawlle myght have with oure
lorde Ihesu, that for love woldè become man dedlye. With hym
y desyrede to suffere, lyevande in dedlye bodye, as god wolde
gyffe me grace.

And in this sodaynlye I sawe the rede blode trekylle downe fro
vndyr the garlande alle hate, freschlye, plentefully, & lyvelye,
ryght as me thought that it was in that tyme that the garlonde
of thornys was thyrstede on his blessede heede. Ryght so both
god and man the same sufferde for me. I conseyvede treulye &
myghttyllye that itt was hymselfe that schewyd it me withowtyn
any meen, and than I sayde, "Benedicite Dominus". This I sayde
reuerentlye in my menynge with a myghtty voyce, and fulle gretlye I was astonnyd for wondere & merveyle that y had that he
wolde be so h[ame]lye with a synfulle creature lyevande in this
wrecchyd flesch[e].

[f.99r] Thus I tokede it for that tyme that oure lorde Ihesu
of his curtayse love walde schewe me comforthe before the tyme
of my temptacyon. For me thought it myght be welle that I schulde, be the suffyrraunce of god and with his kepynge, be temptyd
of fendys or I dyede. With this syght of his blyssede passyon,
with the godhede that I saye in myn vndyrstandynge, I sawe that
this was strengh ynow3e to me, 3e, vnto alle creatures lyevande
that schulde be saffe agaynes alle the feendys of helle & agaynes alle gostelye enmyes.

IV

And this same tyme that I sawe this bodyly syght, oure lorde
schewyd me a gastelye sight of his anly lovynge. I sawe that
he es to vs alle thynge þat is goode and comfortabylle to oure
helpe. He es oure clethynge, for loove wappes vs and wyndes vs,
halses vs and alle be[s]eches vs, + hynges aboute vs for tendyr
loove, that he maye nevere leve vs.

---

16 hamelye] PSS, homblye A.   17 flesche] PSS, fleschly A.   28 anly] homely
CPSS, C adds h- and third minim to -n- to make hamly.   31 beseches] be
teches A, becloseth PSS; vs (2) PS1, vs vs A.

And so in this syght y sawe sothelye that he ys alle thynge
that ys goode, as to myne vndyrstandynge. And in this he schewyd me a lytille thynge the qwantyte of a haselle nutte lyggande
in the palme of my hande, & to my vndyrstandynge that it was as
5 rownde as any balle. I lokede þeropon and thought, "Whate maye
this be?" And I was aunswerde generaly thus, "It is alle that
ys made". I merveylede howe þat it myght laste, for me thought
it myght falle sodaynlye to nought for litille, and I was aunswerde in myne vndyrstandynge, "It lastes and euer schalle, for
10 god loves it, and so hath alle thynge the beynge thorowe the
love of god".

In this lytille thynge I sawe thre partyes. The fyrste is that
god made [it], the seconde ys that he loves it, the thyrde ys
that god kepes it. Botte whate is that to me? Sothelye the
15 makere, the lovere, the kepere. For to I am substancyallye
aned to hym I may nevere have love, reste, ne varray blysse:
that is to saye that [f.99v] I be so festenede to hym that
thare be ryght nought that is made betwyxe my god & me. And
wha schalle do this dede? Sothlye hymselfe, be his mercye &
20 his grace, for he has made me thereto.

And blysfullye restoryd in this god brought owre ladye to myne
vndyrstandynge. I sawe hir gastelye in bodilye lyekenes, a
sympille maydene & a meeke, 3onge of age in the stature that
scho was when scho conceyvede. Also god schewyd me in parte
25 the wisdom & the trowthe of hir saule, whareyn I vndyrstode
reuerente beholdynge, þat sche behelde oure god that ys hir makere, mervelande with grete reuerence that he wolde be borne
of hir that was a sympille creature of his makynge. For this
was hir mervelynge, that he that was hir makere walde be borne
30 of hir that was [made]. And this wysdome [&] trowthe, knawande
the gretnes of hir makere and the lytelleheede of hirselfe that
ys made, made hir [for to] saye mekelye to the angelle Gabri-
elle, "Loo me here, goddys hande maydene."

13 it] CPSS, om A. 26 C adds hyr above oure, oure subpunged. 30 made]
P, a sympille creature of his makynge A, om SS; &] of A, C adds & after
trowthe. 32 for to] C, to PS2, om AS1.

/In this sight I sawe sothfastlye that scho ys mare than alle
þat god made benethe hir in worthynes & in fulheede, for abo-
vene hir ys nothynge that is made botte the blyssede manhede
of criste. This lytille thynge that es made that es benethe
oure ladye saynt Marye, god schewyd it vnto me als litille as
it hadde beene a hasylle notte. Me thought it myght hafe fall-
ene for litille.

In this blyssede revelacyon god schewyd me thre noughtes, of
whilke nou3ttes this is the fyrste that was schewyd me: of
this nedes ilke man & woman to hafe knawynge that desyres to
lyeve contemplatyfelye, that hym lyke to nou3t alle thynge that
es made for to hafe the love of god that es vnmade. For this
es the cause why thaye þat er occupyede wylfullye in erthelye
besynes & euermare sekes warldlye wele er nought he[syd] of
[t]his in herte and in sawlle; for thaye love and seekes here
ryste in this thynge that is so lytille whare no reste ys yn,
& knawes nou3t god that es alle myghtty, alle wyse, and alle
goode, for he is verraye reste.

God wille be knawen, & hym lykes þat [f.100r] we reste vs in
hym. For alle that ar benethe hym suffyces nou3t to vs. And
this is the cause why that na saule ys restede to it be noghthed of alle that es made. When he is noughthid for love to hafe
hym that is alle that is goode, than es he abylle to resayue
gostlye reste.

V

And in that tyme that oure lorde schewyd this that I haue nowe
sayd[e in] gastelye syght, I saye the bodylye syght lastande
of the plentyuouse bledynge of the hede, and als longe as y
sawe that syght y sayde oftyn tymes, "Benedicite Dominus". In
this fyrste schewynge of oure lorde I sawe sex thynges in myne
vndyrstandynge. The furste is þe takyns of his blysfulle passion and the plentevous schedynge of his precyous blode. The
seconde is the maydene, that sche ys his dereworthy modere.

14-15 hesyd of this] he[...] of his A, all in ease PS1, at full ease S2,
C adds -re over erasure. 26 sayde in] PSS, saydene A; C adds in above line;
saye] C inserts saw above line. 30 A inserts þe above takyns.

The thyrde is the blysfulle godhede þat euer was & es & euer
schalle be: alle myghty, alle wysdome, & alle love. The ferthe
is alle thynge that he has made, [for wele I wate that hevene &
erthe & alle that is made] it is mykille & fayre and large &
5 goode. Botte the cause why it [schewed] so lytille to my syght
was for I sawe itte in the presence of hym that es makere. For
to a sawle that sees the makere of alle thynge, alle that es
made sem[es] fulle litylle. The fyfte es that he has made alle
thynge that ys made for love, & thorowe the same love it is
10 kepydde, and euer schalle be withowtyn ende, as it is before
sayde. The sexte es that god is alle thynge that ys goode, &
the goodenes þat $^{+}$ alle thynge has is he.

And alle [þis] oure lorde schewyd me in the fyrst syght, and
gafe me space & tyme to behalde it. And the bodyly syght styn-
15 tyd, & the gastely syght dwellyd in myne vndyrstandynge; & I
abade with reuerente drede, ioyande in that I sawe & desyrande
as y durste for to see mare 3if it ware his wille, or the same
langer tyme.

VI

Alle that I sa[y]e of myselfe I meene in the persone of myne
20 evyncristene, for I am lernede in the gastelye schewynge of
oure lorde that he meenys so. And therfore I praye 3owe alle
for goddys sake, & cownsayles 3owe for 3owre awne profyt, that
3e leve the behaldynge of the wrechid worlde[s] [f.100v] synfulle creature that [it] was schewyd vnto, & that 3e myghtlye,
25 wyselye, lovandlye, & mekelye behalde god that of his curtays
love and of his endles goodnes walde schewe generalye this
visyon in comforthe of vs alle. & 3e that hyerys and sees
this vision and this techynge that is of Ihesu cryste to edi-
ficacyon of 3oure saule, it is goddys wille & my [desyre] that
30 3e take it with als grete ioye and lykynge as Ihesu hadde
schewyd it 3owe as he dyd to me.

3-4 for...made] PSS, om A. 5 schewed] CPSS, om A, C's schewed in right
margin. 8 semes] PSS, semyd A. 12 þat] PSS, þat of A, A inserts þat
above line. 13 þis] CP, these SS, thynge A. 19 saye] PS1, said S2,
sawe A; C inserts alle before myne. 23 worldes] worlde A. 24 it] CPSS,
om A, C adds it above line. 29 desyre] desyrere A.

For the schewynge I am not goode but 3if y love god the better,
and so may and so schulde ylke man do that sees it & heres it
with goode wille and trewe menynge. And so ys my desyre that
it schulde be to euery ilke manne the same profytte that I desyrede to myselfe, & þerto was styrryd of god in the fyrste
tyme when I sawe itte. For yt [is] comon & generale as we ar
alle ane, and I am sekere I sawe it for the profytte of many
oder. For sothly it was nought schewyd vnto me for that god
loves me bettere thane the leste sawlle that is in grace, for
I am sekere thare ys fulle many that nevere hadde schewynge
ne syght botte of the comon techynge of haly kyrke that loves
god better þan I. For 3yf I loke syngulerlye to myselfe I am
ryght nought. Botte in generalle, I am in anehede of charyte
with alle myne evyncristende: for in this anehede of charyte
standes the lyfe of alle mankynde that schalle be safe. For
god is alle that ys goode, and god has made alle that ys made,
& god loves alle that he has made.

And 3yf anye man or woman departe his love fra any of his evyn-
crysten, he loves ryght nought, for he loves nou3t alle; and
so that tyme he ys nou3t safe, for he es nou3t in pees. And
he that generaly looves his evyncrystyn, he loves alle that
es. For in mankynde that schalle be saffe is comprehende alle,
that ys, alle that ys made and the makere of alle. For in
manne ys god, & so in man ys alle. And he þat thus generalye
loves alle his evyncrystene, he loves alle; and he that loves
thus, he is safe. And thus wille I love, & thus I love, and
thus I am safe. For y mene in the person of myne evyncrystene. And the more I love of this lovynge whiles I am here,
the mare I am lyke to the blysse that I [f.101r]⁺ schalle
have in hevene withowten ende, that is god that of his endeles
love wolde become owre brothere & suffer for vs. And I am
sekere þat he that behaldes it thus he schalle be trewly tau3t
& myghttelye comforthtede [if] hym nede comforthe.

Botte god forbede that 3e schulde saye or take it so that I

6 is] om A.   29 that I] that I that I A.   33 if] CPSS, ?A, C adds if
over erasure.

am a techere, for I meene nou3t soo, no I mente nevere so.
For I am a woman, leued, febille, & freylle. Botte I wate
wele this that I saye. I hafe it of the schewynge of hym
tha[t] es souerayne techare. Botte sothelye charyte styrres
5 me to telle 3owe it, for I wolde god ware knawen & myn evyncrystene spede, as I wolde be myselfe, to the mare hatynge
of synne & lovynge of god.

Botte for I am a woman, schulde I therfore leve that I schulde
nou3t telle 3owe the goodenes of god, syne that I sawe in that
10 same tyme that [it] is his wille that it be knawen? And that
schalle 3e welle see in the same matere that folowes aftyr,
[if] itte be welle and trewlye takyn. Thane schalle 3e sone
forgette me that am a wrecche, and dose so that I lette 3owe
nought, & behalde Ihesu that ys techare of alle. I speke of
15 thame that schalle be safe, for in this tyme god schewyd me
no nothere. Bot in alle thynge I lyeve as haly kyrke techis,
for in alle ⁺ this blyssede schewynge of oure lorde I behelde
it as ane in god syght, and I vndyrstode neuer nathynge þereyn
that stonez me ne lettes me of the trewe techynge of halye
20 kyrke.

VII

Alle this blyssede techynge of oure lorde god was schewyd to
me in thre partyes, that is be bodylye syght, and be worde
formede in myne vndyrstandynge, & be gastelye syght. Botte
the gastelye syght I maye nought ne can nought schewe it vnto
25 3owe als oponlye & als fullye as I wolde. Botte I truste in
oure lorde god allemyghtty that he schalle, of his goodnes and
for 3oure love, make 3owe to take it mare gastelye and mare
swetly than I can or maye telle it 3owe, and so motte it be,
for we are alle one in loove.

30 And in alle this I was mekylle styrrede in charyte to myne
evyncrystene that thaye myght alle see and knawe þe same
that I sawe, for I walde that it ware comforthe to thame

---

4 that] thas A. 10 it] _om_ A. 12 if] C, _om_ A. 17 this] PSS, thynge this
A. 27 3owe] _corrected from_ nowe A.

[f.101v] alle as it es to me. For this syght was schewyd in
generalle & nathynge in specyalle. Of alle that [I] sawe,
this was the maste comforthe to me: that oure lorde es so hamlye & so curtayse. And this maste [fil]lyd me with lykynge &
syekernes in saule.

Than sayde I to the folke that were with me, "Itt es todaye
domesdaye with me", & this I sayde for I wenede to hafe dyed.
For that daye that man or woman dyes ys he demyd as he schalle
be withowtyn eende. This I sayde for y walde thaye lovyd god
mare, & sette the lesse pryse be the vanite of the worlde, for
to make thame to hafe mynde that this lyfe es schorte, as thaye
myght se in ensampille be me. For in alle þis tyme I wenede to
hafe dyed.

VIII

And aftyr this I sawe with bodely syght the face of the crucifixe that hange before me, in whilke I behelde contynuely a
party of his passyon: despite, spittynge in, sowlynge of his
bodye, & buffetynge in his blysfulle face; & manye langoures
and paynes ma than I can telle, and ofte chaungynge of coloure,
and alle his blyssede face atyme closede in dry blode. This I
sawe bodylye & hevelye & derkelye, and I desyred mare bodelye
lyght to hafe sene more clerelye. And I was aunswerde in my
resone that ȝyf god walde schewe me mare he schulde, botte me
nedyd na lyght botte hym.

And aftyr this I sawe god in a poynte, that es in myne vndyrstandynge, by whilke syght I sawe that he es in alle thynge.
I behelde with vysemente, wittande and knawande in that syght
that he dose alle that es done. I merveylede in this syght
with a softe drede & thought, "Whate es synne?" For I sawe
trulye that god dothe alle thynge, be itt nevere so litille;
nor nathynge es done be happe ne be eventure, botte the endeles forluke of the wysdome of god. Wharefore me behovede nedes
grawnte that alle thynge that es done es wele done, and I was

2 I] C, om A.   4 fillyd] C, ? slyd A, C ? crosses long s, adds -il-.

sekyr that god dose na synne. [Þerfore it semed to me þat
synne is nouȝt, for in alle thys synne] was nouȝt schewyd me.
And y walde no lengyr mervelle of this, botte behalde oure
lorde whate he wolde schewe me. & in anothyr tyme god schewyd
5 me whate syne es nakydlye be the selfe as y schalle telle
aftyrw[a]rde.

iv /And aftyr this I sawe behaldande the bodye plentevouslye bledande, hate & freschlye and lyfelye, ryȝt as I sawe before in
the heede. And this was schewyd [f.102r] [+] me in the semes of
10 scowrgynge, and this ranne so plenteuouslye to my syght that
me thought ȝyf itt hadde bene so in kynde for þat tyme, itt
schulde hafe made the bedde alle on blode & hafe passede on
abowte. God has made waterse plenteuouse in erthe to oure
servyce and to owre bodylye eese, for tendyr love that he has
15 to vs; botte ȝit lykes hym bettyr that we take fullye his
blessede blode to wasche vs with of synne, for thare ys no
lykoure that es made that hym lykes so welle to gyffe vs, for
it is so plenteuouse and of oure kynde.

v And aftyr this, [or] god schewyd me any wo[r]des, he suffyrde
20 me to behalde langere and alle that I hadde seene & alle that
was thereyn. And than was withowtyn voyce & withowte openynge
of lyppes formede in my sawlle this worde, "Herewith ys the
feende ouercomyn". This worde sayde oure lorde me[n]ande his
passyon, as he schewyd me before.

25 In this oure lorde brought vnto my mynde & schewyd me a perte
of the fendys malyce & fully his vnmyght, and for that he
schewyd me that the passyon of hym is ouercomynge of the fende.
God schewyd me that he hase nowe the same malyce that he had
before the incarnacyon, and als sare he travayles & als con-
30 tynuelye he sees that alle chosene saules eschapes hym wor-

---

1-2 Þerfore...synne (2)] C, and here I saw verely that synne is no dede
for in alle thys synne PSS, om A. C adds omitted line in lower margin,
obelus marks omission point in text. 6 aftyrw[a]rde] a added above o.
9 schewyd] schewyd schewyd A. 19 or] S1, or that P, before S2, houre A;
wordes] PSS, woundes A. 23 menande] menyng PSS, mevande A.

schipfullye, and that es alle his sorowe. For alle that god
suffers hym do turnes [thame] to ioye & hym to payne & to
schame, and he has als mekylle sorowe when god gyffes hym leve
to wyrke as when he werkys nought, and that es for he maye
nevere do als ille as he wolde, for his myght es alle lokene
in goddys hande. Also I sawe oure lorde scorne his malyce
and nought hym, and he wille that we do the same. For this
syght I lugh3 myghttelye, and that made tham to laugh3 that
were abowte me, and thare laughynge was lykynge to me. I
thought y wolde myne evyncristene hadde sene as I sawe; than
schulde thaye alle hafe laughyn with me. Botte I sawe nou3t
cryste laugh3. Neuerthelesse hym lykes that we laugh3 in comfortynge of vs, & er ioyande in god, for the feende ys ouercomyn.

& aftyr this I felle into a saddehete & sayde, "I see thre
thynges: game, scorne, and arneste. I see game that the feende
ys ouercomen, and I see scorne [f.102v] that god scornes hym
and he schalle be scornede, and I see arneste that he es ouercomen be the passion of oure lorde Ihesu cryste & be his dede
that was done ful erneste & with sadde travayle". Aftyr this
oure lorde sayde, "I thanke the of thy servyce & of thy trau-
ayle, & namly in þi 3ough".

IX

God schewyd me thre degrees of blysse that ylke saule schalle
hafe in hevene that wilfullye hase servyd god in any degree
heere in erthe. The fyrste is the wyrschipfulle thankkynge
of owre lorde god that he schalle resayfe when he es delyu-
erede fro payne. This thanke is so hy3e and so wyrschipfulle
that hym thynke it fylles hym þow3 þare ware no mare blys: for
me thought that alle the payne & travayle that myght be suffyrde of alle lyffande men myght nought [hafe] deservede the
thanke that a man schalle hafe that wylfullye has servydde

2 do] A, to do CPSS; thame] vs CPSS, ? A, C adds vs over erasure.
15 I see] APSS, C inserts second I see.   30 hafe] CP, om A.

god. For the seconde, that alle the blyssede creatures þat
er in hevene schalle see that worschipfulle thankynge of oure
lorde god, & he makys his servyce to alle that er in heuen
knawen. And for the thyrde, that als new ande als lykande
5 as it es resayvede that tyme, ryght so schalle itt laste withowten ende: I sawe that goodelye and swetlye was this sayde
& schewyd to me, that þe age of euerylk [man] schalle be knaw-
en in heuen and rewardyd for his wilfulle seruyce and for his
tyme, and namelye the age of thame þat wilfullye and frelye
10 offers thare 3ought vnto god es passande rewardede & wondyrlye
thankkyd.

vii And aftyr this oure lorde schewyd me a souerayne gastelye lykynge in my sawlle. In this lykynge I was fulfillyd of euer-
lastande sekernesse, myghtlye festnede withowtyn any drede.
15 This felynge was so gladde to me and so goodly that [I was] in
peez, in ese, and in ryste, so that þere was nothynge in erthe
that schulde hafe grevyd me. This lastyd botte a while, and
I was turnede & lefte to myselfe in hevynes and werynesse of
myselfe and yrkesumnesse of my lyfe, that vnnethes I cowthe
20 hafe pacyence to lyeve. Thare was none ese ne na comforthe to
my felynge botte hope, faythe, and charyte, and this y hadde
in trowthe botte fulle lytille in felynge.

And anone aftyr, god gafe me agayne the comforth and [f.103r]
the reste in saule, likynge and syekyrnesse so blysfulle & so
25 myghtty þat no drede, no sorowe, no payne bodylye no gastelye
that myght be sufferde schulde have dissesede me. And than
the payne schewyd agayne to my felynge, and than the ioye and
+ the lykynge, & than the tane & nowe the tothere dyverse
tymes I suppose abowte twentye sythes. And in the tyme of
30 ioye I myght hafe sayde with Paule, Nathynge schalle departe
me fro the charyte of cryste. And in payne y myght hafe sayde
with saynte Petyr, Lorde save me, I perysche.

Þis vision was schewyd me to lere me atte my vndyrstandynge

þat it es nedefulle to ylke man to feele on this wyse: sumtyme
to be in comforthe & sumtyme to fayle & be lefte to hymselfe.
God wille that we knowe that he kepes vs euerelyke syekyr in
wele and in woo, & als mykille loves vs in woo as in weele. &
sumtyme, for the profytte of his saule, a man es lefte to hymselfe & to whethere synne es nought the cause. For in this
tyme I synnede nought wherefore I schulde be lefte to myselfe,
ne also I deseruede nou3t to hafe this blysfulle felynge.
Botte frelye god gyffez wele when hym lykes, and suffers [vs]
in wa sumtyme. And bothe es of love: for it is god ys wille
that we halde vs in comforthe with alle oure myght, for blys
es lastande withowtyn ende and payn es passande & schalle be
brought to nought. Therefore it es nought goddys wille that
we folowe the felynges of payne in sorowynge and in mournynge
for tha[im], botte sodaynlye passe on & halde vs in endelesse
lykynge that es god allemyghtty oure lovere & kepare.

X

Aftyr this cryste schewyd me a partye of his passyone nere his
dyinge. I sawe that swete faace as yt ware drye and bludye-
lesse with pale dyinge, sithen mare de[de] pale langourande;
and than turnede more dede to the blewe, & sithene mare blewe
as the flesche turnede mare deepe dede. For alle the paynes
that cryste sufferde in his bodye schewyd to me in the blyssede faace als farfurthe as I sawe it, and namelye in the lyppes.
Thare I sawe this foure colourse, thaye that I sawe beforehande, freschlye & rud[dy], lyflye & lykande to my syght.

This [f.103v] was a hevy chaunge to see this deepe dyinge, and
also the nese c[l]aungede and dryed to my sight. This lange pyn-
ynge semede to me as he hadde bene a seuen nyght dede, allewaye sufferande payne. & me thought the dryinge of crystes
flesche was the maste payne of his passion, and the laste. And
in this dryhede was brou3t to my mynde this worde that cryste

---

9 vs] PSS, om A.   15 thaim] CPSS, C writes final ī over erasure.   19 dede]
CPSS, C adds final -de over erasure.   25 ruddy] CPSS, C adds final -dy
over erasure.   27 claungede] clocggeran togeder P, clange SS, chaungede A.

sayde, "I thryste". For I sawe in criste a doubille thyrste,
ane bodylye, ane othere gastelye. This worde was schewyd to
me for the bodylye thirste, and for the gastelye thyrste was
schewyd to me als I schalle saye eftyrwarde. And I vndyrstode
5 of bodelye thyrste that the bodye hadde of faylynge of moystere, for the blessede flesche & banes ware lefte allane withowtyn blode & moystere. The blyssyd bodye dryede alle ane
lange tyme with wryngynge of the nayles and paysynge of the
h[ede] and weyght of the bodye, with blawynge of wynde fra
10 withoutyn that dryed mare and pyned hym with calde mare than
myn herte can thynke, & alle othere paynes.

Swilke paynes I sawe that alle es to litelle þat y can telle
or saye, for itt maye nouȝt be tolde. Botte ylke saule aftere
the sayinge of saynte Pawle schulde feele in hym þat in criste
15 Ihesu. This schewynge of criste paynes fillyd' me fulle of
paynes, for I wate weele he suffrede nouȝt botte aneȝ, botte
as he walde schewe yt me and fylle me with mynde as I hadde
desyrede before.

/My modere that stode emangys othere and behelde me lyftyd vppe
20 hir hande before me face to lokke myn eyen, for sche wenyd I
had bene dede or els I hadde dyede. And this encresyd mekille
my sorowe, for nouȝtwithstandynge alle my paynes, I wolde nouȝt
hafe been lettyd for loove that I hadde in hym. And to whethere in alle this tyme of crystes presence I felyd no payne
25 botte for cristes paynes, þan thouȝt me I knewe [ful lytylle]
whate payne it was that I askyd. For me thought that my paynes passede any bodylye dede; I thouȝt, "Es any payne in helle
lyke this payne?" And I was aunswerde in my resone that dy-
spayre ys mare for that es gastelye payne. Bot bodilye payne
30 es nane mare than this: howe myght my payne [be more] than to
see hym that es alle my lyfe, alle my blys, & alle mye [f.104r]
ioye suffy[r? Here] felyd I sothfastlye that y lovede criste
so mekille abouen myselfe that me thought it hadde beene a

---

9 hede] C adds -ede over erasure. 25 ful lytylle] P, but litil SS,
fully tylle A. 30 be more] CPSS, om A. 32 suffyr? Here]PSS, suffyrde
hir A.

grete eese to me to hafe dyede bodylye.

Hereyn I sawe in partye the compassyon of oure ladye saynte
Marye, for criste & scho ware so anede in loove that þe gret-
nesse of hir loove was the cause of the mykillehede of hir
payne. For so mykille as scho lovyd hym mare than alle othere,
her payne passed alle othere, and so alle his disciples & alle
his trewe lovers suffyrde paynes mare than thare awne bodelye
dying. For I am sekyr be myn awne felynge that the leste of
thame luffed [hym] mare than thaye dyd thamselfe.

Here I sawe [a] grete anynge betwyx criste and vs, for when
he was in payne, we ware in payne, and alle creatures that
myght suffyr payne soffyrde with hym. And thaye that knewe
hym nou3t, this was thare payne, that alle creatures, sonne &
the mone, withdrewe thare seruyce, and so ware thaye alle
lefte in sorowe for the tyme. And thus thaye that lovyd hym
sufferde payne for luffe, & thay that luffyd hym nought sufferde payne for faylynge of comforthe [of alle] creatures.

In this tyme I walde hafe lokyd besyde the crosse botte I
durste nou3t, for I wyste wele whilys I lukyd vppon the crosse
I was sekyr and safe. Therfore I walde nought assente to
putte my sawle in perille, for besyde the crosse was na sye-
kernesse, botte vglynesse of feendes. Than hadde I a profyr
in my resone as 3yf it hadde beene frendelye. I[t] sayde to
me, "Luke vppe to heven to his fadere". Than sawe I wele,
with the faythe that y felyd, that thare ware nathynge betwyx
the crosse & heuen that myght hafe desesyd me, and othere me
behovyd loke vppe or els aunswere. I answerde & sayde, "Naye,
I may nought, for thowe erte myne heuen". This I sayde for I
walde nou3t, for I hadde levyr hafe bene in that payne to
domysdaye than hafe comen to hevene otherewyse than be hym.
For I wyste wele he that bought me so sare schulde vnbynde me
when he walde.

XI

Thus chese I Ihesu for my heuen wham I [saw] onlye in payne
at that tyme. Me lykede no nothere hevene [f.104v] than Ihesu
whilke schalle be my blysse when I am thare. And this has
euer beene a comforthe to me, that I chesyd Ihesu to my hevene
5   in alle [this] tyme of passyon and of sorowe; and that has
beene a lernynge to me, that I schulde euermare do so and chese
anly hym to my heuen, in wele and in wa. And thus sawe I my
lorde Ihesu langoure lange tyme, for the anynge of the godhede
for love gafe strenght to the manhede to suffyr mare than alle
10 men myght. I mene nought anly mare payne anly than alle men
myght suffyr, bot a[lso] that he suffyrde mare payne than alle
men that euer was fra the fyrste begynnynge to the laste daye.

No tonge maye telle, ne [herte fully] thynke, the paynes that
oure savyoure sufferde for vs, haffande rewarde to the worthy-
15 nes of the hyest worschipfulle kynge and to the schamefulle,
dyspyttous & paynfulle dede. For he that was hieste & worthy-
est was fullyest noghthede & witterlyest dyspyside. Botte the
loue that made hym to suffere alle this, itt passes als fare
alle his payns as heuen es abouen erthe. For the paynes was
20 a dede done in a tyme be the wyrkynge of love, botte luffe
was withowtyn begynnynge, & es and evere schalle be withowtyn
any ende.

And sodaynlye, me behaldande in the same crosse, he chaunchede
into blysfulle chere: the chawngynge of his chere chaungyd
25 myne, and I was alle gladde & mery as yt was possybille. Than
brought oure lorde merelye to my mynde, "Whate es any poynte
of thy payne or of þy grefe?" And I was fulle merye.

XII

ix Than sayde oure lorde, askande, "Arte thou wele payde that I
suffyrde for the?" "3a, goode lorde", quod I. "Gramercy
30 goode lorde, blissyd mut thowe be". "3yf thowe be payede",

---

1 saw] CPSS, ? A, C writes over erasure.　5 this] PSS, om A.　11 also] PSS,
anly A.　13 herte fully] hertefully A.

quod oure lorde, "I am payede. It es a ioye and a blysse and
ane endlesse, lykynge to me that euer y suffyrde passyon for
the, for ȝyf I myght suffyr mare, I walde suffyr".

In this felynge myne vndyrstandynge was lyftyd vppe into heuen,
and thare I sawe thre hevens of the whilke syght I was gretlye
merveylede, and [f.105r] thought, "I sawe thre hevens, and alle
of the blessyd manhede of cryste; and nane is mare, nane is
lesse, nane is hiare, nane is lawere, botte evene like in
blysse".

For the fyrste heuen schewed criste me his fadere, bot in na
bodelye lyknesse, botte in his properte and in his lykynge.
The wyrkynge of the fadere it is this: that he gyffes mede
tille his sone Ihesu criste. This gyfte and this mede is so
blysfulle to Ihesu that [his] fadere myght haffe gyffene na
mede that myght hafe likede hym bettere. For the first heuen,
that is blissynge of the fadere, schewed to me as a heuen, and
itt was fulle blysfulle. For he is fulle blyssede with alle
the dedes that he has done abowȝte oure saluacyon, wharefore
we ere nought anely his thurgh byingge, botte also be the curtayse gyfte of his fadere. We ere his blysse, we er his mede,
we er his wyrschippe, we er his crowne.

This that I saye is soo grete blysse to Ihesu that he settys
atte nought his travayle, and his harde passion, and cruelle
and schamefulle dede. And in this wordes: ȝyf I myght suffyr
mare, I walde suffyr mare, I sawe sothly that ȝif he myght dye
als ofte als fore euerilke man anes that schalle be safe as he
dyed anes for alle, love schulde neuer late hym hafe reste to
he hadde done it. And when he hadde done it, he walde sette
it atte nought for luff, for alle thynge hym botte litylle
in regarde of his love. And that schewed he me wele [sobarly],
sayande this worde: ȝyffe I myght suffere mare. He sayde
nought, ȝif it ware nedfulle to suffyr mare, botte ȝif I myght
suffyr mare. For thowȝ it be nought nedefulle and he myght
suffyr mare, mare he walde. This dede and this werke abowte
oure saluacyon was als wele as he myght ordayne it, it was

14 his] PSS, om̲ A.   27 dyed] A a̲d̲d̲s̲ e a̲f̲t̲e̲r̲ y.   30 sobarly] swetely PSS,
so barly A.

done als wyrschipfullye as cryste myght do it. And in this I
sawe a fulle blysse in cryste, botte this blysse schulde nought
hafe bene done fulle ȝyf it myght any bettere hafe bene done
þan it was done.

5 And in this thre wordes, It is a ioye, a blysse, and ane endeles likynge to me, ware schewed to me thre hevens as thus: for
the ioye I vndyrstode the plesaunce of the fadere; for the
blysse, the wirschippe of the sone; and for the endeles lykynge,
the haly gaste. The fadere is plesed, the sone ys worschippyd,
10 the haly gaste lykes. Ihesu wille that we take heede to this
blysse that is in the blyssedfulle trinite of oure saluacion,
and that we lyke als mekylle [f.105v] with his grace whyles we
er here. And this was schewyd me in þis worde: Erte þow wele
payed?

15 Be the tothere worde that cryste sayde, ȝyf þou be payed I am
payd, he schewed me the vndyrstandynge as ȝyf he had sayde:
It is ioye and lykynge enough to me, and I aske nought els
for my travayle botte that I myght paye the. Plentyuoslye and
fully was this schewyd to me. Thynke also wyselye of the gret-
20 nesse of this worde: That euer I suffred passion for the, for
in that worde was a hye knawynge of luffe and of lykynge that
he hadde in oure saluacion.

XIII

x Fulle merelye and gladlye oure lorde lokyd into his syde and
behelde and sayde this worde, "Loo, how I lovyd the", as ȝyf
25 + he hadde sayde: My childe, ȝyf thow kan nought loke in my godhede, see heere howe I lette opyn my syde, and my herte be clo-
vene in twa, and lette oute blude and watere alle þat was thare-
yn. And this lykes me, and so wille I that it do the. This
schewed oure lorde me to make vs gladde and mery.

xi And with the same chere and myrthe he loked downe on the ryght
31 syde and brought to my mynde whare oure ladye stode in the
tyme of his passion, and sayde, "Wille thowe see hir?" And

25 he] PSS, he he A.

I aunswerde and sayde, "3a goode lorde, gramercy, 3yf it be
thy wille". Ofte tymes I prayed it, and wened to haffe sene
here in bodely lykenes, botte I sawe hir nought soo. And
Ihesu in þat worde schewed me a gastelye syght of hire. Ryght
as I hadde before sene hire litille and sympille, ryght so he
schewed here than, hye and nobille and gloriouse and plesaunte
to hym abouen alle creatures.

And so he wille that it be knawyn that alle tha that lykes in
hym schulde lyke in hire, and in the lykynge that he hase in
hire, and scho in hym. And in that worde that Ihesu sayde:
Wille þou see hire? me thought I hadde the maste lykynge that
he myght hafe gyffen me, with the gastelye schewynge that he
gafe me of hire; for oure lorde schewed me nothynge in specyalle botte oure lady saynte Marye, and here he schewyd me in
thre tymes. The fyrste was as sche consayved, the seconde was
as scho were in hire sorowes vndere the crosse, and the thryd
as scho is nowe: in lykynge, wirschippe, [f.106r] and ioye.

And eftyr this oure lorde schewyd hym to me mare gloryfyed as
to my syght than I sawe hym before, and in this was I lered
that ilke saule contemplatyfe to whilke es gyffen to luke and
seke god schalle se hire and passe vnto god by contemplacion.
And eftyr this techynge, hamelye, curtayse and blysfulle and
verray lyfe, ofte tymes oure lorde Ihesu sayde to me, "I it am
that is hiaste. I it am that þou luffes. I it am that thowe
lykes. I it am that þowe serves. I it am þat þou langes. I it
am that þowe desyres. I it am that thowe menes. I it am þat
is alle. I it am that haly kyrke preches the and teches the.
I it am that schewed me are to the". Thies wordes I declare
nought botte for ilke man, eftyr the grace that god gyffes hym
in vndyrstandynge and lovynge, resayfe tham in oure lordes
menynge.

And eftyr, oure lorde brought vnto my mynde the langynge that
I hadde to hym before. And I sawe that nathynge letted me
bot syn; and so I behelde generallye in vs alle, and me thought,
"3yf syn hadde nought bene, we schulde alle hafe bene clene and
lyke to oure lorde, as he made vs". And thus in my folye, before this tyme, ofte I wondrede why, be the grete forseande

wysdome of god, syn was nought lettede, for than thought me
that alle schulde hafe bene wele. This styrrynge was mekylle
to forsayke, and mournynge and sorowe I made therfore withoutyn resone and dyscrecion, of fulle grete pryde.

5 Neuerthelesse Ihesu in this vision enfourmede me of alle that
me neded. I saye nought that me nedes na mare techynge, for
oure lorde, with the schewynge of this, hase lefte me to haly
kyrke; and I am hungery and thyrstye and nedy and synfulle
and freele, & wilfully submyttes me to the techynge of haly
10 kyrke, with alle myne euencrysten, into the ende of my lyfe.
He aunswerde be this worde and sayde, "Synne is behouelye".
In this worde, Synne, oure lorde brought to my mynde generallye alle that is nought goode: the schamefulle dyspyte and
the vtter noghtynge that he bare for vs in this lyfe and in
15 his dyinge, and alle the paynes and passyons of alle his creatures, gastelye and bodelye. For we ere alle in party noghted,
and we schulde be noghted folowande oure maister Ihesu to we
be fulle purgede, that is to say to we be fully [f.106v] noghted of oure awne dedely flesche, and of alle oure inwarde af-
20 feccion[s] whilke ere nought goode.

And the behaldynge of this, with alle the paynes that euer
ware or euer schalle be, a[lle] this was schewed me in a toch
and redely passed ouere into comforth, for oure goode lorde
god walde noght that the saule ware afferdede of this vglye
25 syght. Botte I sawe noght synne, fore I lefe it has na manere
of substaunce, na partye of beynge, na it myght nought be knaw-
en bot be the paynes that it is cause of. And this payne, it
is sumthynge as to my syght, for a tyme: for it purges vs and
makes vs to knawe oureselfe and aske mercy.

30 For the passion of oure lorde is comforth to vs agaynes alle
this, and so is his blyssyd wille. To alle that schalle be
saffe, he comfortes redely and swetlye be his wordes, and says,
"Botte alle schalle be wele, and alle maner of thynge schalle
be wele". Thyes wordes ware schewed wele tenderlye, schewande

---

19 affeccions] PSS, affeccion A.   22 alle] and alle PSS, and A.

na ma[ne]re of blame to me, na to nane that schalle be safe.
Than were it a grete vnkyndenesse of me to blame or wondyr of
god for my synnes, syn he blames not me for synne. Thus I
sawe howe cryste has compassyon of vs for the cause of synne,
and ryght as I was before with the passyon of cryste fulfilled
with payne and compassion, [lyke in þis I was in party fyllyd
with compassion] of alle myn euencristene; and than sawe I
that ylke kynde compassyone that man hase of his evencristene
with chartye, þat it is criste in hym.

XIV

Bot in this ʒe schalle studye: behaldande generallye, drere-
lye, & mournande, sayande thus to oure lorde in my menynge
with fulle grete drede, "A, goode lorde, howe myght alle be
wele for the grete harme that is comon by synne to thy creatures?" And I desired as I durste to hafe sum mare open de-
clarynge wharewith I myght be hesyd in this. And to this oure
blyssede lorde aunswerde fulle mekelye and with fulle lovelye
chere, and schewed me that Adames synne was the maste harme
that euer was done or ever schalle to the warldes ende, and
also he schewed me that this is opynly [knawyn] in alle haly
kyrke in erthe. Forthermare he lered me that I schulde behalde the gloriouse asethe, for this aseth-makynge is mare
plesande to the blissede godhede and mare wyrschipfulle to
mannes saluacion withowtene comparyson than euer was the
synne of Adam harmfulle.

Þanne [f.107r] menes oure lorde blyssede thus in this techynge, that we schulde take hede to this: "For sen I hafe made
wele the maste harme, it is my wille that þowe knawe þerby
that I schalle make wele alle that is the lesse". He gaffe
me vndyrstandynge of twa partyes. The ta party is oure savi-
our and oure saluacion. This blyssed party is opyn and
clere and fayre and lyght and plentious, for alle mankynde
that is of goode wille or þat schalle be es comprehendyd in

1 manere] PSS, mare A. 6-7 lyke...compassion] CPSS, om A, C adds line
in lower margin, two obeli mark omission point in text. 19 knawyn] PSS,
knawynge A.

this partye. Hereto ere we byddyn of god and drawen and con-
sayled and lered inwardlye be the haly gaste & outwarde by
haly kyrke by the same grace. In this wille oure lorde that
we be occupyed, enioyande in hym, for he enioyes in vs. And
5 þe mare plentyuouslye that we take of this with reuerence and
mekenesse, the mare we deserve thanke of hym and the mare spede
to oureselfe. And thus maye we saye, enioyande, Oure parte
is oure lorde.

The tother parte is spared fra vs and hidde, that is to saye,
10 alle that is besyde oure saluacion. For this is oure lordys
prive consayles [& it langes to þe ryalle lordeschyp of god
for to haue his prive consayles] in pees, and it langes to his
seruauntys for obedyence and reuerence nought to wille witte
his councelle. Oure lorde has pite and compassyon of vs for
15 that sum creatures makes tham so besy þeryn, and I am sekyr
3yf we wyste howe mekille we schulde plese hym and ese oureselfe for to lefe it, we walde. The sayntes in heuen wille
nathynge witte bot that oure lorde wille schewe thame, and
also there charyte and þer desyre is rewlyd eftyr the wille
20 of oure lorde. And þus awe we to wille ne to be lyke to hym,
and than schalle we nathynge wille ne desyre botte the wille
of oure lorde, as he does, for we er alle ane in goddys menynge. And here was I lered that we schalle anely enioye in
oure blissid sauiour Ihesu & trist in hym for alle thynge.

XV

25 /And thus oure goode lorde answerde to alle the questyons and
doutes that I myght make, sayande fulle comfortabelye on this
wyse: "I [maye] make alle thynge wele, I [can] make alle
thynge wele, I [wille] make alle thynge wele, and I [schalle]
make alle thynge wele, and þowe schalle se thyselfe that alle
30 thynge schalle be wele". There he says he maye, I vndyrstande
for the fadere; and þere he says he can, I vndyrstande for the

---

11-12 & it...consayles] CPSS, om A, C adds line in lower margin, obelus
marks omission point in text. 27-28 maye...can...wille...schalle] SS,
may...can...shalle...wylle P, wille...schalle...maye...can A. 29 C inserts
þat above se.

sone; and þer he says [f.107v] I wille, I vnderstande for the
hali gaste; and þere he says I schalle, I vndirstande for the
vnyte of the blyssede trinyte, thre persones in a trewth; &
there he says: Thowe schalle se thyselfe, I vndyrstande the
anynge of alle mankynde that schalle be sayfe into the blysfulle trinyte.

& in this fyve wordes god wille be closed in ryste and in
pees, and thus has the gastely thyrst of cryste ane ende. For
this is the gastely thyrste, the luff langynge, and that lastes
and euer schalle to wee see that syght atte domesdaye. For we
that schalle be safe, and schalle be crystes ioye and his
blysse, ere ȝit here and schalle be vnto the daye. Therefore
this is the thyrste, the falynge of his blysse, þat he has vs
nought in hym als haelye as he schalle thanne haffe. Alle this
was schewed me in the schewynge of compassion, for þat schalle
sese atte domesdaye. Thus he hath rewthe and compassion of vs,
and he has langynge to hafe vs, botte his wysdome and his love
suffers nought the ende to come to the beste tyme.

And in thies same fyve wordes beforesayde: I may make alle
thynge wele, I vndyrstande a myghtty comforthe of alle the
werkys of oure lorde that ere for to come. For ryght as the
blissyd trinyte made alle thynge of nought, ryght soo the same
blyssed trinyte schalle make wele alle that es nought wele.
It is goddys wille that we hafe grete rewarde to alle the
dedys that he has done, for he wille that we knawe thereby
alle that he schalle do, and þat schewyd he me in this worde
that he sayde: And þou schalle see thyselfe that alle manere
of thynge schalle be wele. This I vndyrstande in twa manerse:
ane, I am wele payed that I wate it noght, anothere, I am
gladde and mery for I schalle witte itt. It is goddys wille
that we witte that alle schalle be wele in generalle; botte
it is nought goddys wille that we schulde witte it nowe, botte
as it langes to vs for the tyme: & þat is the techynge of haly
kyrke.

XVI

God schewyd me fulle grete plesaunce that he has in alle men
and women that myghttelye and mekelye and wyrschipfullye takes
the prechynge and the techynge of haly kyrke, for he is haly
kyrke. For he is the grownde, he is the substaunce, [f.108r]
5 he is the techynge, he is the techare, he is the ende, he is
the myddes wharefore ilke trewe sawlle trauaylles. And he is
knawen and schalle be knawen to ylke saule to whame the haly
gaste declares it, and I am sekyr that alle tho that sekes thus
schalle spede, for thay seke god.

10 Alle this that I hafe nowe sayde, and mare that I schalle saye
eftyr, es comforthynge agayne synne. For fyrst, when I sawe
þat god does alle that es done, I sawe nought synne, and than
sawe I that alle is wele. Bot when god schewyd me synne, than
sayde he: Alle schalle be wele.

15 And when god allemyghttye hadde schewed me plentyuouslye &
fully of his goodnesse, I desyred of a certayne person that
I lovyd howe it schulde be with hire. And in þis desyre I
lettyd myselfe, for I was noght taught in this tyme. And than
was I answerde in my reson als it ware be a frendfulle m[ee]n,
20 "Take it generally, and behalde the curtayssy of thy lorde god
as he schewes it to the, for it is mare worschippe to god to
behalde hym in alle than in any specyalle thynge". I assentyd,
and þerwith I lered that it is mare wyrschippe to god to knawe
alle thynge in generalle than to lyke in any thynge in speci-
25 alle. And 3yf I schulde do wysely eftyr this techynge, I
schulde nought be glad for nathynge in specyalle, na desesed
for na manere of thynge, for alle schalle be wele.

God brought to my mynde that I schulde synne, and for lykynge
that I hadde in behaldynge of hym I entendid nought redely to
30 that schewynge. And oure lorde fulle curtayslye abayde to I
walde entende; and than oure lorde brought to mynde with my
synnes the synne of alle myne evencristen, alle in generalle
and nathynge in specialle.

19 meen] PSS, man A.

XVII

Iff alle oure lorde schewyd me that I schulde synne, be me
allayn I vnderstode alle. In this I consayved a softe drede,
and to this oure lorde answerde me thus, "I kepe the fulle
sekerly". This worde was sayde to me with mare love & sekernes of gastely kepynge than I can or maye telle, for as it
was be[f.108v]fore schewed to me that I schulde synne, ryght
so was the comforth schewed to me, sekernesse of kepynge for
alle myne evencristen.

[What may make me mare to luff myne evencristen] than to see
in god that he loues alle that schalle be safe, as it ware
alle a saulle? And in ilke saule that schalle be sayfe is a
goodely wille that neuer assentyd to synne, na neuer schalle.
For as þer is a bestely wille in the nethere party that maye
wille na goode, so is thare a goodely wille in the ouer partye
that maye wille nane eville, botte euer goode, na mare than
the persones of þe blissed trinyte. And this schewyd oure
lorde me in the holehed of luffe that we stande in [in] his
sight, 3a, that he luffez vs nowe als wele whiles we ere here
as he schalle do when we ere thare before his blissed face.

Also god schewed me that syn is na schame, bot wirschippe to
man. For in this sight myn vnderstandynge was lyfted vp into
heven, and than com verrayly to my mynde David, Peter & Paule,
Thomas of Inde and the Maudelayn: howe thaye er knawen in the
kyrke of erth with thare synnes to thayre wirschippe. And it
is to tham no schame that thay hafe synned, na mare it is in
the blysse of heven, for thare the takenynge of synne is turned into wirschippe. Right so oure lorde god schewed me tham
in ensampille of alle othere that schalle cum thedyr.

Syn is the scharpyste scourge that any chosen saule maye be
bette with, whilke scourge it alle forbettes man & woman, and
alle forbrekes [hy]m & noghtez hymselfe in [his] awne syght

9 What...cristen] CPSS, om A, C adds line in top margin, obelus marks
omission point in text. 17 in (3)] PSS, om A. 31 hym] P, tham A; his]
PSS, thare A.

sa fare forth that hym thynke that he is noght worthy bot as
it ware to synke into helle. Botte when contricion takes hym
be the towchynge of the haly gaste, than turnes he bitternesse
into hope of goddys mercye, and than begynnes his woundys to
5 hile and the sawlle to qwykkyn, turnyd in to the lyfe of haly
kyrke. The haly gaste leddes hym to confessyon wilfully to
schewe his synnes, nakedlye & trewly with grete sorowe and
grete schame that he hase swa defowled the fayre ymage of god.
Than he takes pennaunce for ylke a synne, eni[oy]nyd be his
10 domesman, that is growndyd in haly kyrke be the techynge of
the haly gaste. Be this medycyn behoues euer ilke synfulle
sawlle be heled, & namlye of synnes that ere dedely in the
selfe. [f.109r] Thou3 he be heled, his woundes er sene before
god, nowht as woundes bot as wyrschippes. And so on contrarye
15 wyse, as it es punysched here with sorowe and with pennaunce,
it schalle be rewarded in heuen be the curtayse loue of oure
lorde god allemyghttye that wille that nane that comes thare
lese his travayle. That mede that we salle resayfe thare salle
nought be litelle, bot it schalle be hy, gloriouse, and wirschip-
20 fulle, and so schalle alle schame turne into wyrschyppe & into
mare ioye. And I am sekere be myn awne felynge, the mare that
ilke kynde saule sees þis in the kynde & curta[ys]e love of
god, the lathere es hym for to synne.

XVIII

Bot 3yf thowe be styrred to saye or to thynke, sen this is sothe
25 þan ware it goode for to synne for to hafe the mare mede, beware
of this styrrynge and dispice it, for it is of the enmy. For
whate saule that wilfully takys this styrrynge, he maye neuer
be safe to he be amendyd as of dedely synne. For 3if it ware
layde before me alle the payne that is in helle and in purga-
30 torye and in erth, dede and othere and synne, I had leuer chese
alle that payne than synne. For synne is so vyle and so mykille
for to hate that it maye be likened to na payne, whilke payne es
nought syn, for alle thynge is goode botte synne, and nathynge
is wikkyd botte synne. Synne es nowthere deed no lykynge,

9 enioynyd] PSS, eniewnyd A.   22 curtayse] PSS, curtasye A.

botte when a saule cheses wilfully synne that is payne as fore
his god, atte the ende he hase ryght nought. That payne thynke
me the herdeste helle, for he hase nought his god: in alle
paynes a saule may hafe god botte in synne.

And als myghtty and als witty as god is for to safe man, als
willy he is, for criste hymselfe is grownde of alle the lawe
of crysten men, and he has tawht vs to do goode agaynes eville.
Here may we see that he es hymselfe this charite, and does to
vs as he teches vs to do; for he wille that we be lyke to hym
in anehede of endeles luffe to oureselfe and to oure evencristen. Na mare than his love es broken to vs for oure synne, na
mare wille he that oure love be broken to oureselfe ne to oure
evencristen, botte nakedlye hate synne and endeleslye love the
saule as god loves it. For this worde that god sayde es ane
endelesse comforth: that [he] kepes vs fulle sekerlye.

XIX

Aftyr this oure lorde schewed me fo[r] prayers. I sawe ii con-
dicyons in tham that prayes, aftyr that I hafe felyd in myselfe. Ane [f.109v] es, thaye wille nought praye for nathynge
that may be, botte that thynge that es goddes wille and his
wirschippe. Anothere is that thay sette tham myghttelye & contynuely to beseke that thynge that es his wille and his wirschippe, and þat es as I hafe vndyrstandide be the techynge
of haly kyrke. For in this oure lorde lered me the same, to
hafe of goddes gyfte faith, hope, and charyte, and kepe vs
therein to oure lyves ende. And in this we say: Pater noster
aue and crede, with devocion, as god wille gyffe it. And thus
we praye fore alle oure evencristen and for alle manere of
men, that god es wille es, for we walde that alle maner of men
and women ware in the same vertu and grace that we awe to desyre to oureselfe. Botte ȝitt in alle this ofttymes oure
triste is nowht fulle, for we ere nouȝt sekare that god al-
myghtty hyeres vs, as vs thynke for oure vnworthynesse and

6 willy] A alters -ll- from -tt-.   15 he kepes vs] I kepe the PSS, kepes
vs A.   16 for] PSS, foure A.

fore we fele ryght nought. Fore we ere als barayne and als
drye oftymes eftyr oure prayers as we ware before, and thus
in oure felynge oure foly es cause of oure waykenesse, for
thus hafe I felede in myselfe.

5 And alle this brought oure lorde sodaynlye to my mynde, and
myghttely and lyfely, & comfortande me agaynes this maner of
waykenesse in prayers, and sayde, "I am grownde of thy besekynge. First it is my wille that þou hafe it, & s[y]ne I make
the to will it, & syne I make the to beseke it, & ȝif þou be-
10 seke, howe schulde it than be that þou schulde nought hafe thy
besekynge?" And thus in the fyrste reson, with the thre that
folous eftere, oure lorde schewed a myghtty comforth. And the
fy[fte] þare he says: And þowe beseke, thare he schewes fulle
grete plesaunce and endelese mede that he wille gyffe vs for
15 oure besekynge. And in the [six]te reson thare he sais: Howe
schulde it than be þat þou schulde noght hafe thy besekynge,
þare he schewes a sobere vndertakynge, for we tryste nouȝt
als myghtelye als we schulde do.

Thus wille oure lorde that we bath praye & triste, for the
20 cause of the resones beforsayde is to make vs myghty agaynes
waiknesse in oure prayers. For it is goddis wille that we
pray, and þerto he styrres vs in thies wordes beforsayde.
For he wille þat we be sekere to hafe oure prayere, for prayer pleses god. Prayer pleses man with hymselfe, and makes
25 hym sobure & meke that beforehand [f.110r] was in strife &
travayle. Praiere anes the saule to god, for þowȝ the saule
be euer lyke god in kynde and in substaunce, it is oft vnlike
in condicion thurgh syn of mannes party. Than makes prayer þe
saule like vnto god when the sawlle wille as god wille, and
30 than es it lyke to god in condicyon as it es in kynde.

And thus he teches vs to pray and myghttely tryste that we
schalle hafe that we praye fore, for alle thynge that es done
schulde be done þowȝ we neuer prayed it: botte the luff of

---

8 syne] C, sythen PSS, C adds -y- over erasure. 13 fyfte] fyrst APSS.
15 sixte] PSS, fourte C, C alters A's ?sixte by crossing long s-, adding
-our- over erasure.

god es so mykille that he haldes vs parcyners of his goode
deede. And þerfore he styrres vs to praye that [that] hym
lykes to do, for whate prayere or goode wille that we hafe
of his gyfte he wille rewarde vs & gife vs endelese mede, and
this was schewed me in this worde: And þou beseke it.

In this worde god schewed me so grete plesaunce & so grete
lykynge, as ȝif he ware mekille behaldene to vs for ilke
goode dede that we do, alle ȝif it es he that does it. And
for that, we beseke besily to do that thynge that hym lykes,
as ȝif he sayde: Whate myght þowe plese me mare than to bisike
bisily, wisely, & wilfullye to do that thynge that I wille do?

And thus makes prayere accorde betwix god & mannes saule, for
whate tyme that mannes saule es hamelye with god, hym nedes
nought to praye, botte behalde reuerentlye whate he says. For
in alle this tyme that this was schewed me I was noght stirred
to praye, botte to hafe allewaye this welle in my mynde for
comforth, that when we see god we hafe that we desyre, & than
nedes vs nought to praye. Botte when we se nought god, than
nedes vs to pray for faylynge & for habelynge of oureselfe
to Ihesu. For when a saule es tempted, trubled, & lefte to
itselfe be vnreste than es it tyme to pray and to make hymselfe symple and boxsom to god. Bot he be boxom, na maner of
prayer makes god souple to hym. For he is euer ylyke in love;
botte in the tyme that man is in synne, he is so vnmyghttye,
so vnwyse, & so vnluffande that he can nought love god ne hymselfe. The maste myschefe that he hase es blyndnesse, for he
sees nought alle this.

Than the hale luffe of god allemyghty that euer is ane gyffes
hym sight [f.110v] to hymselfe, and than wenes he that god
ware wrathe with hym for his synne. And than is he stirred
to contricion and be confessyon and othere goode dedys to
slake the wrathe of god vnto the tyme he fynde a reste in
saule & softnesse in conscience. And than hym thynke þat god
hase forgyffyn his synnes, and it es soth. And than is god,

2 that (2)] PSS, om A.

in þe sight of saule, turnede in to the behaldynge of the saule,
as ჳif it had bene in payne or in prison, sayande thus: "I am
gladde that þou erte comen to reste, for I hafe euer loved the &
nowe loves the, and þou me". And thus with prayers as I hafe
5 before sayde, & with othere goode werkys þat ere custumab[yll]e
be the techynge of haly kyrke, is þe saule aned to god.

XX

xv   Before this tyme I hadde ofte grete langynge, & desyred of
goddys gyfte to be delyuered of this warlde and of this lyfe,
for I schulde be with my god in blysse whare I hope sikerlye
10 thurgh his mercye to be withowten ende. For ofte tymes I behelde the waa that is here and the weele & the blyssede beynge
thare; & ჳyf thare hadde bene na payn in erthe bot the absence
of oure lorde god, me thouჳt sumtyme it ware mare than I myght
bere. And this made me to mourne & beselye lange.

15 Than god sayde to me for pacience & for sufferaunce thus:
"Sudanly thowe schalle be takene fra alle thy payne, fra alle
thy dissese, & fra alle thy waa; & þowe schalle comen vp abouen, and thowe schalle hafe me to thy mede, and þowe schalle
be fulfyllede of ioye and blysse, & þowe schalle neuer hafe
20 na maner of payne, na maner of sekenes, na maner of myslyk-
ynge, na wantynge of wille, botte euer ioye & blysse withouten
ende. Whate schulde it than greve the to suffyr awhile, sen
it is my wille and my wirschippe?"

Also in this reson: Sudanly þou schalle [be taken], I sawe
25 how god rewardys man of the pacience that he has in abydynge
of goddes wille in his tyme, and þat man lengthes his pacyence
owere the tyme of his lyffynge for vnknawynge of his tyme of
passynge. This is a grete profytte, for ჳif a man knewe his
tyme, he schulde noght hafe pacience owere þat tyme. Also
30 god wille that whiles the saule es in the bodye, that it [seme]
to itselfe that it es euer atte the poynte to be taken. For
alle þis [f.111r] lyfe in this langoure that we hafe here is

___

5 custumabylle] custumabelye A.   24 be taken] PSS, betaken A.   30 seme] P,
semen A.

bot a poynte, and when we ere takene sodaynly oute of payne
into blysse it schalle be nou3t. And þerfore sayde oure lorde:
Whate schulde it than greve the to suffere awhile sen it is my
wille & my wyrschippe?

It is goddys wille that we take his behestys and his confort-
ynges als largelye and als myghtelye as we maye take thame,
and also he wille þat we take oure abydynge and oure desese
als lyghtelye as we may take tham and sette tham atte nought.
For the lyghtlyere we take tham, the lesse price we sette be
tham for luff, the lesse payne salle we hafe in the felynge
of tham, and the mare thanke we schalle hafe for tham.

In this blyssed revelacion I was trewly taught that whate man
or woman wilfully cheses god in his lyfe, he may be sekere
that he is chosene. Kepe this treulye, for sothly it is god ys
wille that we be als sekere in tryste of the blys in heuen
whiles we ere here as we schulde be in sekernesse when we ere
thare. And euer the mare likynge and the ioye that we take in
this sekernesse with reuerence and mekenes, the bettere likes
hym, for I am sekyr 3if thare hadde nane ben bot I that schulde
be safe, god wolde hafe done alle that he hase done for me.

And so schulde ilke saule thynke in knawynge of his lovere,
forgettande 3if he myght alle creatures, & thynkkande that god
hase done for hym alle that he hase done. And thys thynke me
schulde styrre a saule for to luff & lyke hym, & nought drede
bot hym, for it is his wille that we witte that alle the myght
of oure enmye is loken in oure frendes hande. And þerfore a
saule that wate sekerly this schalle nought drede botte hym
that he loves, and alle othere dredes sette tham emange passyons and bodelye sekenesse & ymagynacions.

And þerfore 3if a man be in so mekylle payne, in so mekylle waa,
& in so mekylle deseses, that hym thynke that he can thynke
ryght nought bot that þat he es in or that he feles, als sone
as he maye, passe lyghtlye owere and sette it atte nou3t. And
why? For god wille be knawen. For 3yff we knewe hym & luffed
hym, we schulde hafe [f.111v] pacience and be in grete reste,
& it schulde be lykynge to vs alle that he does. And this
schewed oure lorde me in thies wordes þat he sayde: Whate

schulde it than greve the to suffyr awhile sen it is my wille
and my wirschippe? And here was ane ende of alle þat oure
lorde schewed me that daye.

XXI

And efter this sone I felle to myselfe & into my bodelye sek-
5 nes, vnderstandande that I schulde life, & as a wrech ⁺ heuyed
and mourned for the bodely paynes that I feled, and thou3t
grete irksumnes that I schulde langere lyffe. And I was als
barane and drye as 3if I hadde neuer had comforth before bot
litille, for fallynge to my paynes & faylynge of gastelye fel-
10 ynge. Than com a religiouse person to me and asked me howe I
farde, and I sayde that I ha[dd]e raued þat daye; and he lugh
lowde & enterlye and I sayde, "The crosse that stode atte my
bedde feete, it bled faste". And with this worde the person
that I spake to wex alle sadde & meruelande, and onane I was
15 sare aschamed for my reklessenes, & I thou3t thus: "This man
takys it sadlye the leste worde that I myght saye, that says
na mare þerto".

And when I sawe that he toke it so sadelye & with so grete
reuerence, I wex ryght gretly aschamed and walde haffe bene
20 schryfen. Bot I couth telle it na preste, for I thought,
"Howe schulde a preste leue me? I leued nought oure lorde
god". This I leued sothfastlye for the tyme that I sawe hym,
and so was than my wille & my menynge euer for to do withowten ende. Bot as a fule I lette it passe fro my mynde. Loo,
25 I, wrich! This was a grete synne & a grete vnkyndnes that I,
for folye of felynge of a litille bodelye payne, so vnwyselye
lefte for the tyme the comforth of alle this blissede schewynge of oure lorde god. Here maye 3e see whate I am of myselfe, botte herein walde nought oure curtayse lorde leue me.

30 And I laye stille tille nyght, tristande in his mercye, and
than I beganne to slepe. And in my slepe, atte the begynnynge,
me thought the fende sette hym in my throte and walde hafe
strangelede me, botte he myght nought. Than I woke oute of

5 wrech] P, wretch I SS, wrech that A.   11 hadde] PSS, hafe A.

my slepe, & vnnethes hadde I my lyfe. The persones that ware
with me behelde me and wette my temples, and my herte began
to comforth, and onane a lytelle smoke come in atte the dore
with a grete hete [f.112r] and a fowle stynke. I sayde, "Benedicite dominus! Is alle on fyre that is here?" And I wened it
hadde bene a bodely fyre that schulde hafe brenned vs to dede. I
asked tham that ware with me 3yf thaye felyd any stynke. Thay
sayde Naye, thay felyd nane. I sayde, "Blissede be god", for
than wiste I wele it was the fende was comen to tempest me.
And onane I tuke þa that oure lorde hadde schewed me on the
same daye with alle the fayth of hali kyrke, for I holde it
as bathe ane, & fled þerto as to my comforth. And alsone
alle vanysched awaye, & I was brought to gret reste and pees
withoutene seknes of bodye or drede of conscyence.

                              XXII

Bot than lefte I stylle wakande, and than owre lorde openedde
my gastely eyen & schewyd me my saule in myddys of my herte.
I sawe my saule swa large as it ware a kyngdome, and be the
condicions that I sawe þerin, me thought it was a wirschip-
fulle cite. In myddys of this cite sittes oure lorde Ihesu,
verraye god & verray man, a fayre persone and of large stature, wyrschipfulle, hiest lorde: and I sawe hym cledde sol-
emplye in wyrschippes. He sittes in the saule euen ryght in
pees & reste, and he rewles & 3emez heuen & erth and alle that
is. The manhede with the godhede sittis in reste, and the godhede rewles & 3emes withowtyn any instrumente or besynes; and
my saule [is] blisfullye occupyed with the godhede that is
sufferayn myght, sufferayne wisdome, sufferayne goodnesse.
The place that Ihesu takes in oure saule he schalle neuer
remove it withowtyn ende, for in vs is his haymelyeste hame
& maste lykynge to hym to dwelle in.

This was a delectabille syght & a restefulle, for it is so in
trowth withowten ende, and the behaldynge of this whiles we
ere here es fulle plesande to god, and fulle grete spede to
vs. And the saule that thus behaldys it makys it lyke to hym

26 is] PSS, om A.

that is behaldene, and anes in reste & in pees. And this was
a singulere ioye & a blis to me that I sawe hym sitte, for
the behaldynge of this sittynge schewed to me sikernes of his
endelesse dwellynge. And I knewe sothfastly that it was he
5 that schewed me [f.112v] alle before.

And when I hadde behalden this with fulle avisement, than
schewed oure lorde me wordys fulle mekelye, withowtyn voyce
& withowten openynge of lyppes, as he hadde done before, and
sayde fulle soberlye, "Witte it welle, it was na rauynge that
10 thowe sawe today. Botte take it, and leue it, and kepe þe
therto, and þou schalle nought be ouercomen". This laste wordes ware sayde to me for lernynge of fulle trewe sikernes,
that it is our lorde Ihesu that schewed me alle. For ryght
as in the fyrste worde that oure lorde schewed me, menande
15 his blissyd passion: Herewith is the fende ouercomen, ryght
so he sayde in the laste worde, with fulle trewe sikernesse:
Thow schalle nought be ouercomen.

And this lernynge and this trewe comforthe, it es generalle
to alle myne euencristen as I haffe before sayde, & so is
20 goddys wille. And this worde, Thowe schalle nought be ouercomen, was sayde fulle scharpely and fulle myghtely for sekernes and comforth agayne alle tribulacions that maye com. He
sayde nought [þou salle not] be tempestyd; thowe schalle not
be trauayled; þou schalle not be desesed. Bot he sayde: Þou
25 schalle nou3t be ouercomen. God wille that we take hede
of his worde and that we be euer myghtty in sekernesse, in
wele and in waa. For he luffes vs and likes vs and so wille
he that we luff hym and lyke hym and myghtely triste in hym,
and alle schalle be wele. And sone eftyr alle was close &
30 I sawe na mare.

XXIII

After this the fende com agayne with his heete and with his
stynke & made me fulle besye. The stynke was so vile and so

---

10 A adds þe above line. 23 þou salle not] om A, added by C in right margin.

paynfulle, and the bodely heete also dredfulle & trauaylous;
& also I harde a bodely iangelynge & a speche, as it hadde
bene of two bodyes, and bathe to my thynkynge iangled at anes
as 3if thay had haldene a parliamente with grete besynes. And
alle was softe mutterynge, and I vnderstode nou3t whate thay
sayde, botte alle this was to stirre me to dispayre as me
thou3t. And I triste besely in god & comforthede my sawlle
with bodely speche as I schulde hafe done to anothere person
than myselfe that hadde so bene travaylede. Me thought this
besynes myght nought be [f.113r] lykned to na bodely besenes;
my bodelye ey3en I sette on the same crosse that I hadde sene
comforth in before that tyme, my tunge I occupyed with speche
of cristes passion & rehersynge of the faith of hali kyrke,
and my herte I festende on god, with alle the triste and alle
the myght that was in me.

And I thou3t to myselfe, menande, "Thowe hase nowe grete besynes; walde þou nowe fra this tyme euermare be so besy to kepe
the fro synne, this ware a soferayne & a goode occupacion".
For I trowe sothlye, ware I saffe fra synne, I ware fulle saife
fra alle the fendes of helle & enmyse of my saule. And thus
thay occupied me alle the nyght, and on the morn tille it was
aboute pryme dayes. And than onane thay ware alle gane and
passed, and þere lefte nathynge bot stynke and that lasted
stille a while. And I scorned thame and thus was I delyuered
of tham be the vertu of cristes passion: for tharewith is the
fende ouercomen, as criste sayde before to me.

A, wriched synne! Whate ert þou? Thowe er nought. For I sawe
that god is alle thynge: I sawe nought the. And when I sawe
that god hase made alle thynge, I sawe the nought; and when
I sawe that god is in alle thynge, I sawe the nought; and
when I sawe that god does alle thynge þat is done, lesse and
mare, I sawe the nought. And when I sawe oure lorde Ihesu
sitt in oure saule so wyrschipfully, & luff and lyke and rewle
and 3eme alle that he has made, I sawe nou3t the. And thus
I am sekyr þat þou erte nou3t; and alle þa that luffez the and
lykes the and folowes the and wilfully endes in the, I am
sekyr thay schalle be brought to nought with the, and endles-
lye confownded. God schelde vs alle fra the. Amen par charyte.

And whate wrecchednesse is I wille saye, as I am lernede be
the schewynge of god. Wrecchydnesse es alle thynge that is
nought goode: þe gastelye blyndehede that we falle into in the
fyrste synne, and alle that folowes of that wrecchydnesse,
5 passions & paynes, gastelye or bodely; and alle that es in erth
or in othere place whilke es nouȝt goode. And than may be
asked of this: Whate er we? [f.113v] And I answere to this:
ȝif alle ware departed fra vs that is nouȝt goode, we schulde
be goode. When wrechidnesse is departed fra vs, god and the
10 saule is alle ane, and god and man alle ane.

Whate is alle in erthe that twynnes vs? I answere and saye:
In þat that it serues vs it is goode, and in that that it
schalle perisch it [is] wricchednes, and in that that a man
settys his herte þeropon othere wyse than thus it is synne.
15 And for þat tyme that man or woman loves synne, ȝif any be
swilke, he is in payne that passes alle paynes. And when he
loves nouȝt synne, botte hates it and luffez god, alle is wele.
And he that trewlye doez thus, þowȝ he syn sum tyme by frelty
or vnkunnynge in his wille, he falles nought, for he wille
20 myghtely ryse agayne & behalde god wham he loves in alle his
wille. God has made tham to be loved of hym or hire that
has bene a synnere, bot euer he loves, and euer he langes to
hafe oure luffe. And when we myghttelye and wisely luffe
Ihesu, wee er in pees.

25 Alle the blissede techynge of oure lorde god was schewed to
me be thre partyes as I hafe sayde before, that es to saye be
the bodely sight, and be worde formed in myn vndyrstandynge,
& by gastelye syght. For the bodely sight I haffe sayde as I
sawe als trewlye as I can, and for the wordes fourmed I hafe
30 sayde tham ryght as oure lorde schewed me thame. And for the
gastely sight I hafe sayde somdele, bot I maye neuer fully
telle it. And þerfore of this gastely sight I am stirred to
say more, as god wille gyfe me grace.

13 is] om A.

XXIV

God schewed me twa maners of sekenes that we hafe, of whilke
he wille that we be amended. The tone es inpacyence, for we
bere our trauaylle and oure payne heuely. The tothere is dispayre o[r] doutefulle drede as I schalle saye efterwarde. And
thiese twa er it that moste travayles vs and tempestes vs, as
by that oure lorde schewed me, and maste lefe to hym that
thiese be amendede. I speke of swylke [f.114r] men and women
that for goddes love hates synne and dysposes tham to do goddes wille: than ere thiese twa priue synnes, and maste besye
aboute vs. Therefore it is goddys wille that thay be knawen,
and than schalle we refuse tham as we do othere synnes.

And thus fulle mekelye oure lorde schewed me the pacience that
he hadde in his harde passyon, and also the ioye and the lykynge that he hafes of that passion for love. And this he
schewed me in ensampille, that we schulde gladlye & esely
bere oure paynes, for that es grete plesynge to hym & endelesse profitte to vs. And cause why we ere travayled with
tham is for vnknawenge of luffe.

Þowȝ the persones in the blissede trinyte be alle even in properte, luffe was moste schewed to me, that it is moste nere
to vs alle, and of this knawynge er we moste blynde. For
many men and women leues that god is allemyghty & may do alle,
and that he is alle wisdome and can do alle; botte that he is
alle love & wille do alle, þar thay stynte. And this vnknawynge it is that most lettis goddes luffers, for when thay be-
gyn to hate synne, and to amende tham by the ordynnaunce of
holye kyrke, ȝit þere dwelles a drede that styrres tham to
behaldynge of thamselfe and of þer synnes before done. And
this drede þay take for a mekenesse, bot this is a fowlle
blyndehede and a waykenesse; and we can it nouȝt dispyse, for
ȝif we knewe it þa[n] we schulde sodaynly dispice it, as we

---

4 or] PSS, of A.   14 this] erasure between i and s.   21 A adds of above
line.   31 þan] þat A, þat subpunged.

do ane othere synne þat we knawe, for it comes of the enmy &
it is agayne the trewthe.

For of alle the propertees of the blissed trinite, it is goddes wille that we hafe moste sekernesse in lykynge and luffe.
5 For luffe makes myght & wisdome fulle meke to vs; for ryght
as be the curtasye of god he forgettys oure synne for tyme we
repente vs, right so wille he that we foregette oure synne,
and alle oure hevynesse, and alle oure dowtefulle dredes.

XXV

[f.114v] Fore I saw foure maner of dredes. One is drede of
10 afray that comes to a man sodanly be frelty. This drede is
good, for it helpes to purge a man, as does bodely seknes or
swylke odere payne that is nought synne; for alle swylke paynes helpes man ȝif thay be paciently taken. The secunde is
drede of payne, wharby a man is styrred & wakned fro slepe of
15 syn. For man þat is harde in slepe of syn, he is nouȝt able
for þe tyme to resayfe the soft comforth of the hali gaste,
to he hafe getyn this drede of payne of bodely dede & of the
fyre of purgatory; and this drede styrres hym to seke comforth
and mercy of god. And thus this drede helpys hym as ane antre,
20 and ables hym to hafe contricion be the blysfulle t[o]chynge
of the hali gaste. The thyrde is a doutfulle drede, for þowȝ
it be litille in the selfe & it ware knawen, it is a spice of
dispayre. For I am sekyr that alle doutefulle dredes god hates,
and he wille þat we hafe tham departed fro vs with trewe knaw-
25 ynge of l[uf]fe.

The fourthe is reuerente drede, for þare is na drede that
pleses hym in vs bot reuerente drede, and that is fulle swete
and softe for mekillehede of luffe. And ȝit is this reuerente
drede and luffe nought bathe ane, bot thay er twa in properte
30 and in wyrkynge, & nowthere of tham may be hadde withowtyn
othere. Therfore, I am sekyre, he þat luffez he dredes, þowȝ
he fele bot litille. Alle dredes othere than reuerente dredes
that er proferde to vs, þowȝ thay come vndere the coloure of

20 tochynge] PSS, techynge A.   25 luffe] lyfe A.

halynes, thay ere not so trewe. And hereby may thaye be knawen and discerned whilke is whilke: for this reuerente drede, the mare it is hadde, the mare it softes and comfortes & pleses and restes, and the flase drede it travayles and tempestes & trubles.

Than is this the remedye, to knawe tham bath & refuse [þ]e fals, righte as we walde do a wikkyd spiritte that schewed hym in liknes of a goode angelle. For ryght as ane ille spyrit, þow3 he com vndere the coloure and the liknes of a goode angelle, his daliaunce & his wirkynge þow3 he schewe neuer so fayre, fyrst he travayles & tempes[tes] & trubles the person that he spekes with, and lettes hym and lefez [f.115r] hym alle in vnreste, and the mare that he comonez with hym, the mare he travayles hym, and the farthere is he fra pees. Þerfore it is goddes wille and oure spede that we knawe tham thus ysundure, for god wille euer that we be sekere in luffe, & peessabille & ristefulle as he is to vs. And ryght so of the same condicion as he is to vs, so wille he that we be to oureselfe, and to oure evencristen. Amen.

Explicit Iuliane de Norwych

---

6 þe] PSS, 3e A.   11 tempestes] tempes A.   20 Explicit rubricated.

NOTES

7-8   **bodelye syekenes**: according to the author of the
Cloud (p.80), physical illness was an obstacle to
contemplation; "þerfore for Godes loue beware wiþ
seeknes as moche as þou maist goodly, so þat þou be
not þe cause of þi febilnes".

12   Cf. the Cloud (chaps. 16-23) for a discussion of Mary
Magdalene, "in persone of alle sinners þat ben clepid
to contemplative liif", as the greatest of Christ's
lovers; also Luke vii.47, x.42.

15-6   **Notwithstandynge** that **I** leevyd (and Nouȝtwithstondynge
alle this trewe beleve, 39/21): Julian is anxious lest
her desire to experience Christ's suffering be inter-
preted as lack of faith.

9   **ryghtynges** (also 41/6): cf. rightes PS2, rites S1; OED
lists right (sb.2) as an erroneous spelling for 'rite',
but does not record Julian's form.

14   **tempestes** 'perturbation' (OED tempest sb.2).

15   **othere paynes**: the pains of the fiends, "dredes & tempestes", have just been cited; now Julian asks that
she also be allowed to experience any other pains asso-
ciated with dying.

    safe: Julian wishes to be brought to the point of death,
but not actually to die.

24   **ȝought**: Julian desired the sickness in her youth. A's
error may originally have been the result of þ/ȝ confusion; cf. 52/10.

26   St. Cecilia was martyred for her refusal to worship the
pagan gods. The first attempt to kill her, by boiling,
was a failure. This was followed by an attempt to de-
capitate her in the bath, with three blows to the neck;
there she lingered half dead for three days, a detail
reminiscent of the initial three-day period of Julian's
sickness (41/5-6) as the three blows recall the "thre
woundys" (39/8-9); see the Bibliotheca Hagiographica
Latina, Nos. 1495, 1496, cited by Bryan and Dempster
(1958:667ff.), and Windeatt (1977:12-3).

32   **wounde**: Julian has desired three wounds; the first is
the wound of contrition. Possibly the corruption was
suggested by the plural in the previous line.

33   **wylfulle langgynge to god**: cf. the Cloud (p.15) "Alle
þi liif now behoueþ algates to stonde in desire....
Þis desire behoueþ algates be wrouȝt in þi wille, bi
þe honde of Almiȝti God & þi consent".

11   **lothe thouȝt** 'it seemed hateful' (OED think, v.1,B.1).

15   **I myght**: sense requires the addition, and PSS support
it.

41/18   wolde lyeve: the PSS reading, "had leued", reflects the historical perspective of the longer version, while A has the immediacy of a recent experience.

42/8ff.   The darkness that surrounds Julian in her chamber is comparable to that described in the Cloud (p.16-7): "at þe first tyme...þou fyndest bot a derknes, and as it were a cloude of vnknowyng...þerfore schap þee to bide in þis derknes...for ʒif euer schalt þou fele him or see him...it behoueþ alweis be in þis cloude & in þis derknes".

42/12   huglye 'ugly'.

42/22   derne: PSS suggest the solution to A's nonsense reading.

43/4   dedlye 'mortal' (OED deadly, a.1); cf. "a mortal man", S2.

43/7   In the longer version Julian provides a description of each of the sixteen shewings: "The first is of his precious crownyng of thornes and ther in was conteined and specified the blessed trinitie with the incarnacion and the vnithing betweene god and mans sowle" (P f.1r).

43/12-3   withowtyn any meen: cf. the Cloud (p.7) "God ʒeueþ þis grace freely with outen any mene, &...it may not be comen to wiþ menes". (OED mean, sb.2, II.9.c, "a mediator between God (or Christ) and man").

43/14   reuerentlye in my menynge 'with reverent intent'. Julian's controlled reaction to the first of her shewings recalls the Cloud's advice to avoid acting wildly (chap.46) and to suspect extraordinary signs (chap.48).

43/16   hamelye: cf. 49/3, 59/22.

43/17   flesche: A errs elsewhere in the process of changing folios (46/23, 47/29, 50/9); cf. "dedely flesche" (60/19).

43/23   saye: PSS read saw, but saye is a regular 13th-16th-century past indicative form.

43/28   anly 'peerless', 'preëminent' (OED only, a.5).

43/30   wappes 'wrap', 'envelop' (OED wap, v.2, to 1542; PSS substitute wrappeth).

43/30-2   He es...leve vs: cf. the Book (p. 156), "vncloþe þi-self of al maner of felyng of þi-self, þat þou be able to be cloþid wiþ þe gracyous felyng of God self ...Oure Lorde...seiþ [I] am þe side garnement of loue & of lastyng þat neuer schal haue eende".

43/31   halses 'embrace' (OED halse, v.2 and MED halsen v.[2]).

          beseches 'lay siege to' (OED besiege v.1); cf. becloseth PSS (OED beclose, v., 'to enclose', 'imprison'): as A elsewhere shows mixed evidence of voicing and unvoicing (section 3b), I here follow the closest spelling to A, and that likely to explain the source of the error.

vs: one vs is otiose in A.

15   to 'until' (OED to, conj. c.l); cf. till PSS.

17   I be so festenede: the sense of 'until' is to be understood from initial "For to".

21   restoryd 'replace (mankind) in a state of grace' (OED restore v.4.a); Julian's vision of the hazel nut has shown her the extent of God's love, and comforted, she moves to the next stage of the revelation, the vision of "owre ladye".

23   ȝonge of age: PSS add that she was "little waxen aboue a chylde" (P f.8v).

30   made: reference to P provides the reading necessary to correct A's dittography.

    wysdome & trowthe: according to A's own testimony (44/25), this is the correct reading; C, providing the needed ampersand, has mistakenly placed it after trowthe.

32   for to: in A make is regularly constructed with the infinitive (cf. 45/12, 48/27, 49/11, 51/8, 56/18).

33   Luke i.38, "Dixit autem Maria: Ecce ancilla Domini".

2   fulheede 'fullness' (OED fullhead), 'abundance', 'plenty' (MED fulhed(e); cf. the Scale "In hyr [the Virgin] was fulhede of all vertues without wem of synne" (III,22: quoted in OED).

8   thre noughtes: "hym lyke to nouȝt alle thynge that es made" (45/11-2); "[thaye]...knawes nouȝt god (45/17); "alle that ar benethe hym suffyces nouȝt to vs" (45/20).

14-5   hesyd of this: reference to PSS provides the evidence needed to repair A's corruption. A's form of the verb 'ease' is hesyd (61/15).

21   noghthed 'to set (one) at nought' (OED nought, v.l).

24   PSS here add more than two full chapters. Julian expounds on the meaning of the revelation—"to lerne our soule wisely to cleue to the goodnes of god" (P f.10v)—and on how prayer, as a means of cleaving to God, pleases him. She continues with a description of Christ's bleeding head, which image has been present to her during the entire course of the first Revelation. The "grett droppes of blode felle...lyke pelottes...the plentuoushede is lyke to the droppes of water that falle of the evesyng of an howse after a grete shower of reyne...and for the roundnesse they were lyke to the scale of heryng in the spredyng of the forhede" (P f.14r,v). The section ends with a discussion of the "marvelous homelynesse" of God's love (P f.16r).

26   sayde in: A's error may result from a fusion of sayde in to form saydene.

46/3-4   made...made: A's omission, unnoticed by C, may result from homoeoteleuton. Because this is a relatively common error in A (cf. 50/1-2, 61/6-7, 65/9), and only one line is involved, I supply P's reading. However, in the case of 72/32 (see Note) A's putative omission seems too extensive to justify reinstatement.

46/6-8   Reynolds (1952:21) compares this passage to one from St. Gregory's Life of St. Benedict, "quia animae videnti Creatorem angusta est omnis creatura".

46/8   semes: the present tense is here required.

46/13   alle þis: A's error was perhaps suggested by the occurrences of "alle thynge" twice in the preceding two lines.

46/19   saye: A's error may result from saye/sawe confusion (43/23n), but sawe is not recorded as a legitimate preterite form of say.

46/27   sees 'understand' (OED see, v. B.3); Julian's evyncristene do not see the vision themselves: through her they understand it generally (cf. 47/2).

47/1   For the schewynge...the better: the 14th-century mystics generally agree that witnessing extraordinary phenomena is not itself proof of holiness; PSS add, "and in as much as 3e loue god the better it is more to 3ow than to me" (P f.18r).

47/6   is: sense requires the addition.

47/8ff.   For Julian's disclaimer cf. 2 Corinthians xii.5.

47/13   anehede 'oneness', 'a community' (OED onehead, onehood, 1,2).

47/14   evyncristende: possibly an East Midlands form = 'equally baptized'.

47/18ff. Cf. 1 John iv.8, "Qui non diligit non novit Deum, quoniam Deus caritas est", and 1 John iv.20, "Si quis dixerit quoniam diligo Deum, et fratrem suum oderit, mendax est".

47/29   that I: A's dittography has occurred in the process of changing folios.

47/34   Julian's disclaimer, omitted in PSS, is stirred by the contemporary furor over women as preachers. Reynolds (1958:310) points to the Book of Margery Kempe (Meech, 1961:259, 6/9n; 315, 126/14n); cf. 1 Corinthians xiv. 34, 1 Timothy ii.12).

48/4   that: A's error may result from anticipation of the subsequent es.

48/10   it: sense requires the addition

48/13   dose: the form is 14th-century northern, 2nd plural imperative (OED do, A.2.d.ծ).

48/17   in alle this: possibly A's error was suggested by the occurrence of "in alle thynge" in the preceding line.

18   god syght: see Mustanoja (1960:72) for the mainly northern use of the s-less genitive with proper names and personal nouns; cf. criste 54/15.

19   stonez: the closest OED definition is 'break', 'crush' (stun, v.4), but Julian's sense is less literal: nothing that she has seen could be spiritually harmful.

18-20 and I...kyrke: in the longer version Julian omits this sentence, but adds that "the feyth of holy chyrch which I had before hand...stode contynually in my syghte"(P f.19r).

23-5   Cf. 2 Corinthians xii.4 "Quoniam raptus est in paradisum, et audivit arcana verba quae non licet homini loqui". By "maye nought ne can nought" Julian means not only that her modest powers are unequal to the task, but that it is not permitted. Cf. Hilton, Of Angels' Song (Horstmann, 1895: I,775): "Bot what [Aungells] sange es, it may noghte be dyscryuede be no bodyly lyknes, for it es gastely, and abown all manere of ymagynacyone and mans reson".

1-2   For this syght...specyalle: cf. the Book (p.142), "[the Passion of Christ] was in general & not in specyal, wiþ-outyn special beholdyng to any o man in þis liif, bot generaly & in comon for alle".

14   "The secunde is of þe discoloring of his fayer face in tokenyng of his deerworthie passion" (P f.1r).

14ff. Cf. Matthew xxvii.30, Luke xxii.64.

15   hange: OED (hang, v.A.2.n) records hang as a regular northern preterite form from the 13th century on.

16   despite 'scorn' (OED despite, sb.1), 'humiliation', 'insult', 'outrage' (MED despit, n.3).

       in 'on' (OED in, prep. I.2).

       sowlynge 'defiling' (see OED sowl, v.1).

17   langoures 'sorrows' (OED languor sb.3).

19   and alle...dry blode: the longer version here goes into greater detail: "halfe the face begynnyng at the ere over 3ede with drye bloud tyll it closyd in to the myd face and after that the other halfe beclosyd on the same wyse" (P f.19v).

20   hevelye 'with difficulty' (OED heavy, a.1).

22-3   Cf. Apoc. xxi.23, "Lucerna eius est agnus"; also The Anglo-Norman Voyage of St. Brendan (Waters, 1928: 1.325-6), "quant ço Deus li volt mustrer/ Sur ço ne stout cirge alumer".

23   This is the end of the second Revelation in A, but PSS add a long passage before the beginning of the third (P f.20r-22v): Julian describes the paradox of her desire, "And thus I saw him and sought him and I had hym and wantyd hym" (cf. Song of Solomon iii.1, "In lectulo meo per noctes quaesivi quem diligit anima

mea; quaesivi illum et non inveni".) She includes
an image showing that man is safe as long as God is
with him, "One tyme my vnderstandyng was lett downe
in to the sea grounde and ther saw I hilles and dales
grene semyng as it were mosse begrowyng with wrake and
gravell; Then I vnderstode thus that if a man or woman wer there vnther the brode water...he shoulde be
safe in sowle and body and take no harme".

49/24   "The third is that our lord god almightie all wisdom
and all loue right also verily as he hath made all
thinges that is right also verilie he doeth and wor-
kith all thinges that is done" (P f.1r).

And aftyr this...vndyrstandynge: cf. Bishop Ullathorn
quoted by Butler (1927:39), "There is but one point in
the universe where God communicates with us, and that
is the centre of our own soul", and the Book (p. 141),
"Þe poynte of þi beholding is moste substancialy set
in þe naked siȝt & þe blynde felyng of þin owne being"
Reynolds (1952:24) compares the passage to one of Dio-
nysius the Areopagite, "All the radii of a circle are
concentrated into a single unity in the centre, and
this point contains all the straight lines brought together within itself and unified to one another, and
to the one starting point from which they began" (she
quotes from The Divine Names and Mystical Theology of
Pseudo-Dionysius, trans. C.E.Rolt, London, 1920:137).

49/26   vysemente 'consideration', 'attention' (OED advisement,
sb.1), 'reflection' (MED avisement, n.2(a)). Cf. 74/6.

49/28   softe drede: cf. 65/2 and chap. XXV.

49/30   botte 'without' (OED bout, B. prep. 2).

49/31   forluke 'providence' (OED forelook, sb.b), 'foresight',
'divine providence' (MED for(e-lok, n.(2)).

50/1-2 synne...synne: A's error results from homoeoteleuton.

50/7   "The iiiith is skorgyng of his tender bodie with plen-
tuous sheding of his precious bloud" (P f.1r-v).

50/8-9 ryȝt...heede: see 43/7ff. PSS include a longer and mor
detailed description of the "feyer skynne...broken full
depe into the tendyr flessch with sharpe smytynges all
about the sweete body" (P f.25r).

50/9   schewyd: A's dittography occurs in the process of turn
ing folios.

semes 'on the face or body: a long incised wound' (OED
seam, sb.1, I.4.b).

50/19   "The vth is that the feende is overcome by the precious
passion of Christ" (P f.1v). PSS conclude the fourth
Revelation with references to the Harrowing of Hell
and the Ascension, "...this precious plenty of hys
dere worthy blode it descendyd downe into helle and
brak her bondes...[it] ascendyth vp into hevyn in the
blessed body of our lord Iesu crist" (P f.26r-v).

or god...wordes: confusion between houre and or could result from dictation; the woundes/wordes error involves a simple confusion of two visually similar words. A's woundes is improbable, since God has just finished showing Julian his wounds (50/7ff.); and directly after this vision, words are formed in her soul: "herewith ys the feende ouercomyn" (50/22-3).

0/23   menande: cf. 74/14; the error originated from a misreading of the u/v minim set.

1/2   thame: the space left by C's erasure is large enough for this word, which, following the "chosene saules", fits the context.

1/5-6   lokene in goddys hande: cf. 71/26.

1/7   nought hym 'set him at nought'; the longer version reads "nowghtyng hys vnmyght".

1/16   arneste 'intense passion' (OED earnest, sb.1,1), 'vehemence of feeling or action', 'ardor or fury, as in conflict' (MED ernest, n.4(a)).

1/23   "The vith is the worschipfull thangking of our lord god in which he rewardyth all his blessed seruauntes in heauen" (P f.1v).

PSS precede this section with one describing God's "solempne fest" provided in heaven for "alle his derewurthy frendes"; "I saw hym ryally reigne in hys howse and all fulfyllyth it with ioy and myrth" (P f.29r); (cf. The Dream of the Rood, "... þær is blis mycel/ dream on heofonum, þær is Dryhtnes folc/ ȝeseted to symle...", Dickins and Ross, ed., London, 1954: 11.139-41).

1/30   hafe deservede: sense requires that C's addition be retained.

2/3   he makys his: God makes the soul's.

2/7-8   þe age...in heuen: Reynolds (1956:311) compares this passage to one of St. Thomas, "Secundo ostendit exemplar hujus perfectionis (i.e. resurgentium) cum dixit: 'In mensuram aetatis plenitudinis Christi'" (Commentarium in Ep. S. Pauli ad Ephesios, lectio IV, Marietti Edition, Turin, 1929:50).

2/12   "The viith is often tymes feeling of wele and of wooe feeling of wele is gracious touching and lightnyng with true sekernes of endless ioy the feeling of woo is of temptation by heauenes and werines of our fleshely liuyng with ghostely vnderstanding þat we be kept also verily in loue in woo as in wele by the goodnes of god" (P f.1v).

2/18-9   hevynes and werynesse of myselfe; yrkesumnesse of my lyfe: these feelings afflict Julian when the "souerayne gastelye lykynge" has been taken from her; Reynolds compares the experience to St. John of the Cross' Night of the Senses (1956:xxxv).

52/26ff. And than the payne...and than the ioye...& than the
          tane & nowe the tothere: cf. the Book (p. 168), "siþ
          he sumtyme goþ & somtyme comeþ...By þe wiþdrawyng of
          þi feruour, þe whiche þee þenkeþ his goyng, þof al it
          be not so, wole he properly proue þi pacyence"; also
          the Scale (p. 11), "But this feeling in his fervour
          cometh not alway when a man would nor it lasteth not
          well long. It cometh and goeth as he will that giv-
          eth it...when it is withdrawn dread not too mickle,
          but stand in faith and in a meek hope, with patient
          abiding till it come again".

52/28   the lykynge: A's error, suggested by the than...than
          structure of the sentence, opposes "the lykynge" to
          "the ioye"; in fact they belong together, in oppo-
          sition to "the payne".

52/30-1   Cf. Romans viii.35, "Quis ergo nos separabit a cari-
          tate Christi?"

52/32   Cf. Matthew viii.25, "Domine salua nos perimus", and
          xvi.30 "Domine salvum me fac".

53/3ff.   Cf. Isaiah liv.7, "In modico dereliqui te, et in mo-
          mento indignationis meae percussi te, et in misera-
          tionibus meis multis congregabo te".

53/6   & to whethere: possibly an unrecorded form of though
          whether (OED, adv., 'nevertheless', 'however'); cf.
          54/23-4.

53/9   vs: sense requires the addition.

53/17   "The viiith is the last paynes of Christ and his cruel
          dying" (P f.1v).

53/24-5   beforehande: in the first Revelation.

53/27   claungede: cf. OED clang, v.2, 'to clag', 'render stiff
          OED clag, v., 'to clog with anything sticky'; MED clin-
          gen, v., 'to stick together, congeal, harden'. A's
          error, which involves the confusion of a single letter,
          is revealed by reference to PSS.

          PSS include a more detailed description of the drying
          of the flesh: "blodlessehed and payne dryed with in
          and blowyng of the wynde and colde comyng from with
          out and the payne dryede vppe alle the lyuely spyrites
          of cristes flessch thus I saw the swete flessch dry in
          my syght parte after perte dryeng with mervelous payne"
          (P f.32v-33r).

53/28   dede 'on the verge of death'; PSS add "at the poynt
          of out passing". Julian, too, lingered at the point
          of death for seven nights (41/4ff.).

54/1   Cf. John xix.28, "Sitio".

54/4   eftyrwarde: at 63/7ff.

54/10   pyned hym with calde: cf. Þe Wohunge (p.283), "þat
          luuelike bodi þat henges swa rewli...swa kalde".

/11   PSS include more details of the crucifixion, "for tendyrnes of the swete handes and the swete feet... the woundys waxid wyde"; the crown was "bakyn with drye blode with the swet here clyngyng the drye flessch to the thornys". The passage continues with a fuller description of the tearing of the flesh by the thorns, and of the "iiii maner of dryeng" (P ff.33v-35r).

/14   the sayinge of saynte Pawle seems obscure, but Harford and Reynolds compare the phrase to Philippians ii.5, "Hoc enim sentite in vobis, quod et in Christo Iesu", Harford citing the Wyclif translation, "and fele ye this thing in you: which also in crist ihesus". Cf. also Acts xvii.28, "In ipso enim vivimus et movemur et sumus", and 1 Corinthians vi.17, "Quid adheret Deo, vnus spiritus est cum illo" (quoted in "A Pistle of Prayer", Deonise Hid Divinite, 1955:56).

/23   lettyd: prevented from seeing the crucifix.

/25   ful lytylle: A's error results from incorrect word-division.

/30-2   howe myght...suffyr: cf. Þe Wohunge (p.283), "A hu liue i for reowðe þat seo mi...lefmon up o rode?"

/32   suffyr? Here: A's error possibly results from confusion of the homophones here and hir. A's hir may have gone uncorrected because it begins a folio and is followed by a passage describing the "compassyon of oure ladye", "hir loove" and "hir payne" (55/2ff.).

/11   alle creatures: PSS explain more fully: "alle creatures that god hath made to oure servys þe fyrmamente and erth feylyd for sorow in ther kynd in the tyme of cristes dyeng" (P f.36v).

/12-3   thaye that knewe hym nouȝt: the longer version mentions that there are "ii maner of people" in this category, understood by "ii persons": "Pylate", and "seynt dyonisi of france whych was that tyme a paynym" (P f.37r).

/13-4   Cf. Matthew xxiv.29, "Statim autem post tribulationem dierum illorum, sol obscurabitur et luna non dabit lumen suum"; also Mark xiii.24, and The Prick of Conscience, 1. 4702 (Morris, 1863) on the subject of "þe day of dome": "Takens sal be in þe son and in þe mone, And in the sternes...in heven".

/18ff.   In this tyme: this passage seems at variance with the fact that Julian's mother has just closed her eyes (54/19-21).

/22   profyr 'a proposal' (OED proffer, s.1).

/5   this: Julian refers specifically to the vision she has just experienced.

/10   anly mare payne anly: possibly PSS omit the second anly for stylistic reasons, but A's sense stands:

'not only more pain (singly) than all men (together) might suffer'.

56/11   also: A's third <u>anly</u>, perhaps suggested by the two immediately preceding, must be otiose. Cf. "nought anely...botte also" (57/19).

56/13   No <u>tonge</u>...<u>thynke</u>: cf. þe <u>Wohunge</u> (p. 281), "Bute hwat tunge mai hit telle. hwat heorte mai hit þenche ...of alle þa buffetes...þat tu þoledest"; "hart may thyngk or tong may telle" (P f. 152r); 1 Corinthians ii.9; <u>Roman de la Rose</u> 1.2965; <u>The Merchant's Tale</u>, [IV (E) 1341].

56/14   <u>rewarde</u> 'regard', 'consideration' (<u>OED</u> <u>reward</u>, sb.1, I.1; from 1338 to 1475: PSS read <u>regard</u>). Cf. 63/24.

56/17   <u>witterlyest</u> 'certainly', 'truly' (<u>OED</u> <u>witterly</u>, adv., to 1500: P reads <u>vtterly</u>, SS <u>utterlyest</u>.

56/27   PSS make the optimistic ending of the revelation more explicit: "we shal be with hym in hevyn...and than shall alle be brought in to ioy...and we shalle be fulle of blysse...and for this lytylle payne that we suffer heer we shall haue an hygh endlesse knowyng in god...the harder oure paynes...the more shalle our worshchppe be with hym in his kyngdom" (P ff.41r-v)

56/28   "The ixth is of þe lykyng which is in the blessed trinite of þe hard passion of Christ after his ruwfull dying in which ioy and lykyng he will þat we be in solace and myrth with hym tylle that we come to the glorie in heauen" (P ff.1v-2r).

       <u>payde</u> 'satisfied', 'pleased' (<u>OED</u> <u>pay</u>, v.1,1).

56/30   <u>mut</u> 'may', used in wishes (<u>OED</u> <u>mote</u>, v.1, 1.c).

57/5   <u>thre hevens</u>: see 58/5ff.

57/11   <u>properte</u> 'essential quality' (<u>OED</u> <u>property</u>, sb.5,6).

57/16   <u>blissynge</u> 'giving of joy' (<u>OED</u> <u>bliss</u>, v.2).

57/17   <u>blyssede</u> 'gladdened' (<u>OED</u> <u>bliss</u>, v.1).

       <u>he</u>: Ihesu; to clarify, PSS substitute <u>Iesu</u> for the second he in the sentence.

57/19   <u>byingge</u>: see 55/31.

57/24   <u>this wordes</u>: see 57/3.

57/24ff. Cf. <u>Ancrene Wisse</u> (Tolkien, 1962:200), "ne mahte he wið leasse gref habben arud us? ȝeoi iwiss ful lihtliche . ah he nalde . for hwi?....Me buð lihtliche þing þat me luue lutel. He bohte us wið his heorte blod: deorre pris nes neauer . forte ofdrahen of us ure luue toward him . þat costnede him se sare".

57/29   <u>thynge</u> 'seem' (<u>OED</u> <u>think</u> v.1, A.1.).

57/31   PSS expound more fully on the meaning of Christ's willingness to die as often as he might: "Thys is the hyghest profer that our lorde god myght make to mannes

soule...and heer saw I...the loue that made hym to
suffer it [the passion] passith as far alle his paynes
as hevyn is aboue erth" (P f.43v).

7/35   als wele: the sense of 'ordained' must be understood
before A's als wele; PSS read "ordeyned as wele".

8/5   this thre wordes: see 57/1-2.

8/13   þis worde: see 56/28.

8/15   the tothere worde: see 56/30-57/1.

8/19   PSS here describe the "propyrte of a gladde geauer",
whose joy comes from having "plesyd and solacyd hym
that he lovyth" (P f.45v).

8/20   this worde: see 57/2.

8/23   "The x is our lord Iesu shewyth by loue his blessed
hart clouen on two" (P f.2r).

8/23-4   oure lorde...the: cf. Ancrene Wisse (p.200), "openin
his side . to schawin hire his heorte to schawin hire
openliche hu inwardliche he luuede hire . & to ofdrahen hire heorte". Also Þe Wohunge (p.283), "A
swete ihesu þu oppnes me þin herte for to cnawe witer-
liche...for þer i mai openlich seo hu muchel þu me
luuedes".

8/27   Cf. John xix.34, "Sed unus militum lancea latus eius
aperuit, et continuo exivit sanguis et aqua". Also
Þe Wohunge (p.283), "he [Longinus] þurles his side
cleues tat herte . and cumes flowinde ut of þat wide
wunde þe blod þat bohte . þe water þat te world wesch
of sake and of sunne". In Þe Wohunge this passage is
followed by the phrase "Lauedi moder and meiden þu
stod here ful neh and seh al þis sorhe"; and in the
Revelations the shewing of the blood and the water
is followed by the sight "whare oure ladye stode in
the tyme of his passion" (58/31-2).

8/30   "the xi is an high ghostly shewing of his deer worthy
mother" (P f.2r).

        chere 'joy' (OED cheer, sb.4) or 'countenance' (sb.2).

8/32   Wille thowe see hir: PSS explain that in this question
are implicit two others: "wylte thou se how that I
loue her?" and "wylt thou se in her how thou art louyd?"
(P ff.47v, 48r).

9/18   "The xii is that our lord god is all souereyn being"
(P f.2r).

9/23ff. Cf. Ancrene Wisse (p.202-3), "Nam ich þinge feherest .
nam ich kinge richest . nam ich hest icunnet . nam
ich weolie wisest . nam ich monne hendest . nam ich
þinge freoest?...nam ich alre þinge swotest & swetest?"

9/26   menes 'aim at', 'direct one's way to' (OED mean, v.1,c).

9/27   alle: cf. Colossians ii,9, "Quia in ipso [Christ] inha-
bitat omnis plenitudo divinitatis corporaliter".

59/28 are 'before' (OED ere, A. adv., 4); P reads before.

59/32 "The xiiith is that our lord god will that we haue great regard to all the deedes which he hath done in the great noblete of all thyng makyng...than meaneth he thus behold and see for by the same myght wisdom and goodnes I shall make well all that is not well..." (P ff. 2r-v).

60/8 Cf. Matthew v.6, "Beati qui esuriunt et sitiunt iustitiam, quoniam ipsi saturabuntur".

60/11 behouelye 'useful', 'profitable' (OED behovely, a).

60/19 affeccions: the plural is required.

60/22 alle: PSS suggest the solution to A's problematical reading.

61/1 manere: reference to PSS reveals A's error, possibly the result of a failure to expand an abbreviated form.

61/6-7 compassion...compassion: A's error results from homoeoteleuton.

61/7 An amplification in PSS explains that trials are sent by God to those who are to be saved in order to keep them from "pompe", "pryde", and "the veyne glorye of thys wrechyd lyffe"; and that the contemplation of the immeasurably greater suffering of Christ will save them from "grugyng and despeyer" (P ff.52r,v).

61/10 studye 'meditate' (OED study, v.I, 2).

61/11-2 in my...drede 'in a spirit of great dread'.

61/18 ever schalle: the sense of 'be done' carries over from the preceding 'was done'.

61/21 asethe 'reparation' (OED asseth(e), sb), (MED asseth n, 1(a)); cf. The Prick of Conscience (Morris, 1863: 1.3610), "Thurgh asseth makyng, Als thurgh penance", and the Cloud (p.31), "I schulde make asseþ".

62/9-14 The tother parte...his councelle: cf. The English Writings of Richard Rolle (Allen, 1931: XI, 43), "It es presumpsion, a man by his awen wytt for to prese to mekill into knawyng of gastly thynges".

62/11-2 consayles...consayles: A's omission results from homoeoteleuton.

62/20 to wille...hym: Julian asks that we not repeat Adam's sin by seeking knowledge that is God's alone.

62/27-8 maye...can...wille...schalle: cf. 62 /30-63/3, where Julian interprets her own passage; the order corresponds with the hierarchy of father, son, holy ghost, and unity of the trinity (according to A the order would be an unlikely holy ghost, trinity, father, and son). Also cf. 63/19-20, where Julian repeats the first phrase of the series, "I may make alle thynge wele".

63/7 this fyve wordes: see 62/27ff.

/14   PSS add a passage discussing the ways in which "crist
Iesu is both god and man" (P ff.55v-56v): as he is
divine, he is the highest, "glorifyed and vnpassible",
but as he is human, he suffers; "ruth and pyte" are
divine qualities, "thurst and longyng" human ones (cf.
63/16ff.).

/6   myddes 'means' (OED mids, A. sb.2).

/11   fyrst: to clarify, PSS add "in the thyrde schewyng".

/16   a certayne person: Julian's question about the welfare
of a particular friend is not answered; cf. the Cloud's
teaching that the contemplative should hold no man in
special regard (chap. 24).

/19   meen: cf. 43/12-3, where the revelation is "schewyd...
withowtyn any meen".

/1   Iff alle 'although' (OED if, conj. I.8.a); also alle
3if 69/8.

/8-9   evencristen...cristen: A's omission results from homoeoteleuton.

/11ff.   That in "ilke saule that schalle be sayfe" there is
a portion of the will that never consents to evil is
the one possibly unorthodox point that Julian raises.
Perhaps she refers to a division such as that described
in the Cloud between the "principal" (spiritual) and
the "secundary [physical] mi3tes" (chap. 62ff.). Earlier the Cloud's author remarks that sin "is bot ve-
nial" if "þe grounding & þe rotyng of 3oure entent [is]
in God", and this recalls the Scale (p.368), "The common grace lasteth whole whatsoever a man do, as long
as his will and his intent is true to God, that he
would not sin deadly". Reynolds (1952:26) compares Julian's passage to Eckhart: "the spark of the soul is
[God's] light...the reflection of his divine nature
and ever opposed to anything ungodly" (she quotes from
The Works of Meister Eckhart, trans. C.deB.Evans,
London, 1924: I,88).

/17   in in: A, thinking the second in otiose, omits.

/23   Julian's point is that these prominent figures are
all famous for their sins: David for his passion for
Bathsheba and the death of Uriah (2 Samuel xi); Peter
for the denial (Matthew xxvi.69-75); Paul for assist-
ing at the martyrdom of St. Stephen (Acts vii.58);
Thomas for doubting the resurrection (John xx.25-8);
Mary Magdalene for being a prostitute (Luke vii.37).

/29   Molinari (1958:80,1n.) draws attention to a strikingly
similar passage in the Scale in which Hilton describes
the "second conversion": "At the beginning of his conversion a man...generally dwells most on his sins. He
feels great compunction and sorrow...And if he is
strongly touched with compunction, because God wishes
to cleanse him quickly, his sins will seem to be always in his sight, and to be so foul and horrible that

he hardly knows what to do....God works in some men's hearts in this way....He must first cleanse him by making him feel the fire of compunction for the great sins he has committed" (quoted from Sitwell, 1953:49).

65/31   hym...his: there is no reason to preserve A's singular plural confusion, corrected in PSS.

66/9   enioynyd 'to impose a penalty...esp. of a spiritual director' (OED enjoin, v), 'esp. to prescribe or impose penance' (MED enjoinen, v).

66/34   lykynge 'desire' (OED liking, vbl.sb. 1,2.b).

67/5-6   als myghtty...als willy: cf. the Book (p.161-2), "He [God] is my3ty, witty & willy enow3 to do þe best for þee".

67/13-4   nakedlye hate...the saule: cf. the Cloud (p.65), "dede may leuefully be demyd, bot not þe men, wheþer þei ben good or yuel"; and the Scale (p.65), "But it is a great mastery for a man to be able to love his even-christian in charity and wisely hate the sin of him and love the man".

67/15   he kepes vs: cf. 65/3-4 "I kepe the fulle sekerly", the worde to which Julian refers.

67/16   "The xiiii is that our lord god is grownd of our beseking hear in was seen two fayer properties...rightfull preaier...[and] verie trust...and thus our praier liketh him and he of his goodnes fullfillyth it" (P f.2v).

68/1-2   als barayne and als drye: cf. the Book (p.167), "boþe þese euidence [inner and outer]...sese for a tyme, & þou be lefte as þou were bareyn".

68/11   the fyrste reson: "I am grownde of thy besekynge".

the thre that folous: "it is my wille"; "I make the to will it"; "I make the to beseke it".

68/13   fyfte: Julian has just discussed the first four reason next in the sequence must be the fifth and the sixth (68/15). With the first four he shows "a myghtty comforth" (68/12); with the fifth he shows "fulle grete plesaunce and endelese mede" (68/13-4); and with the sixth he shows "a sobere vndertakynge" (68/17).

69/2   that that 'for that which'; A mistakenly omits the second that, but cf. 71/32, 76/12.

69/5   this worde: see 68/13.

69/19   habelynge 'an act of preparing oneself' (MED ablinge, ger.); see also OED able, v.1, and cf. the Cloud (p.2), "for to able him to contemplatiue leuyng", and Rolle (Parry, 1921:20), "tille oure soule be somewhat... abiled to gostely werke".

69/22   symple 'devoid of pride', 'humble' (OED simple, a.A.2).

69/23   souple 'soft', 'tender' (OED supple, a.1).

70/5   custumabylle 'customary' (OED customable, a.1).

/7   "The xv is that we shuld sodeynly be takyn from all our payne and from all our woo and of his goodnes we shall come vppe aboue wher we shall haue our lord Iesu to our meed and for to be fulfilled with ioy and blisse in heauen" (P f.2v).

/24   this reson: see 70/16.

/30   seme: the singular form is required.

/2   The longer version here adds a striking image: "And in thys tyme I sawe a body lyeng on þe erth whych body shewde heuy and feerfulle and withoute shape and forme as it were a swylge stynkynge myrre and sodeynly oute of this body sprong a fulle feyer creature a lyttle chylld full shapyn and formyd swyft and lyfly and whytter then the lylye whych sharpely glydyd vppe in to hevyn. The swylge of the body betokenyth grette wretchydnesse of oure dedely flessch and the lyttylnes of the chylde betokenyth the clennes and the puernesse of our soule" (P f.138r).

/22   forgettande...alle creatures: cf. the Cloud (p.24), "put a cloud of for3etyng bitwix þee & alle þe cretures þat euer ben maad".

/5   heuyed 'to be moved or agitated in mind', 'to feel vexation' (OED heave, v. B.II,12).

/12   enterlye 'heartily' (OED entire, adv. B.4.a); 'wholeheartedly' (MED enterli, adv. 1(a)).

/31-2   Cf. 2 Corinthians xii.7, "et ne magnitudo revelationum extollat me, datus est mihi stimulus carnis meae, angelus Satanae ut me colaphizet".

/32   the fende: PSS include a detailed portrait of the fiend: his face was "lyke a yonge man and it was longe and wonder leen...the coloure was reed lyke tylle þe tylle stone whan it is new brent with blacke spottes thare in lyke frakylles fouler than þe tyle stone his here was rede as rust...he grynnyd vpon me with a shrewde loke shewde me whyt teth...body ne handes had he none shaply but with hys pawes he helde me in the throte" (P f.142v). The fact that this passage begins after the worde throte (72/32) and ends with the same word admits the possibility that it was in A's exemplar, and was omitted because of homoeoteleuton.

/15   "The xvi is that the blessed trinitie our maker in Christ Iesu our sauiour endlesly dwelleth in our sowle worschipfully rewlyng and comaunding all thinges vs mightly and wisely sauyng and kepyng for loue and we shall not be overcome of our enemy" (P f.2v-3r).

         lefte 'remained' (OED leave, v.1, III.12).

/23   3emez 'governs' (OED yeme, v.3); 1400 is the last date cited in OED, and P seems not to recognize the word, substituting 3evyth.

73/25   besynes 'trouble', 'difficulty' (OED business, I.7); but cf. 75/4, where it means 'activity' (I.2). Also 75/7 where besely = 'earnestly', 'fervently' (OED busily, adv. 2) and 74/32 where besye = 'anxious' (OED busy, a.6). At 75/10, 75/16-7 besynes = 'occupation' (though not of a bodily sort), and at 75/17 besy = 'occupied' (OED busy, a.1).

73/31ff. This was...in pees: cf. 2 Corinthians iii.18, "Nos vero omnes revelata facie gloriam Domini speculantes, in eandem imaginem transformamur".

73/31   it 'itself'.

74/2-4   I sawe...dwellynge: cf. Boece Book V, Prosa 3 (Robinson 1957:375): "For certes yif that any wyght sitteth, it byhoveth by necessite that the opynioun be soth of hym that conjecteth that he sitteth..."; Boethius uses the image in his discussion of necessity, Julian uses it to affirm the "sikernes of his endelesse dwellynge".

74/14   the fyrste worde: formed during the fifth Revelation (50/22-3).

74/21   scharpely 'distinctly' (OED sharply, adv. 7).

74/23   þou salle not. A's omission may result from homoeoteleuton.

75/5   softe mutterynge: PSS here insert a note comparing the muttering to a mock-telling of the rosary, "semyng to me as they scornyd byddyng of bedys whych are seyde boystosly with moch faylyng devout intendyng and wyse diligence" (P ff.146v - 147r).

75/7   I triste besely: cf. The Parson's Tale (cited as a representative tract on the deadly sins) [X(I)683] (Robinson 1957), "Accidie...loveth no bisynesse at al".

        triste: OED (trist, v.1) notes that from the 13th-15th centuries a contracted preterite form is usual.

75/16-8   Thowe...occupacion: cf. The Parson's Tale [X(I)713], "An ydel man is lyk to a place that hath no walles; the develes may entre on every syde".

75/26   as criste sayde before: in the fifth Revelation; the words of Christ have proven true in Julian's own experience.

76/13   is: sense requires the addition.

76/21   tham: "that man or woman" (76/15).

76/26   as I hafe sayde before: see 48/22-3.

77/2   inpacyence: PSS read "vnpacyens or slouth".

77/4   or: cf. 78/21, where it is clear that doubtful dread is a type of, and thus an alternate name for, despair. Cf. The Parson's Tale on Accidia [X(I)692], "now comth wanhope, that is despair of the mercy of God...thurgh which despeir or drede he abaundoneth al his herte to every maner synne".

77/27   <u>drede</u>: morbid dwelling on past sins can be wrongly
seen as contrition. See chap. XXV, where the first
and second "maner of dredes" can be positive in their
effect; and cf. the <u>Cloud</u>, chap. 31, where the author
argues that contemplation of past sins can come between the soul and God.

77/31   <u>þan</u>: C wanted to deleʈe A's <u>þat</u>; A probably intended
to write <u>þan</u>.

78/8   <u>hevynesse</u>: the Parson [X(I)685]uses the same word:
"Accidie is lyk hem that been in the peyne of helle,
by cause of hir slouthe and of hire hevynesse".

78/19   <u>antre</u> 'a means or way of entrance' (<u>OED</u> <u>enter</u>, sb.1);
'a means of entering or attaining to' (<u>MED</u> <u>entre</u>, n.
6 (b)). <u>OED</u> and <u>MED</u> do not record A's spelling, but
<u>MED</u> lists <u>anter-</u> as an AF variant of the prefix <u>enter-</u>.

78/20   <u>tochynge</u>: cf. 66/2-3.

78/21   Cf. Julian's words to Margery Kempe (Meech 1951:42),
"He þat is euyr-mor dowtyng is lyke to þe flood of
þe see, þe whech is mevyd & born a-bowte wyth þe
wynd, & þat man is not lyche to receyuen þe ȝyftys
of God".

78/25   <u>luffe</u>: it is knowledge of love, not life, that will
free us from "doutefulle drede".

79/11   <u>tempestes</u>: cf. 73/9 and 79/4-5, "travayles and tempestes & trubles".

BIBLIOGRAPHY

Allen, H.E., ed., English Writings of Richard Rolle, Hermit of Hampole (Oxford, 1931).

Bazire, J., "The Dialects of the Manuscripts of the Chastising of God's Children", JEGP, 6 (1957), 64-78.

Blomefield, F.P.C., An Essay Towards a Topographical History of the County of Norfolk (London, 1805-10).

British Museum, The Catalogue of Additions to the Manuscripts in the British Museum 1906-10 (London, 1912).

Bryan, W.F. and Dempster, G., ed., Sources and Analogues of Chaucer's Canterbury Tales (New York, 1958).

Butler, C., Western Mysticism (London, 1927).

Chambers, P.F., Juliana of Norwich: an Introductory Appreciation and an Interpretive Anthology (London, 1955).

Clay, R.M., The Hermits and Anchorites of England (London, 1914).

Coleman, T.W., English Mystics of the Fourteenth Century (London, 1938).

Colledge, E., and Bazire, J., ed., The Chastising of God's Children and the Treatise of Perfection of the Sons of God (Oxford, 1957).

Colledge, E., and Walsh, J., "Editing Julian of Norwich's Revelations: a Progress Report", Medieval Studies, 38 (1976), 404-27.

_____ ed., A Book of Showings, Toronto Studies and Texts, 35 (Toronto, at press). [P]

Darwin, F.D.S., The Medieval Recluse (London, 1940).

Davis, N., "The Language of the Pastons", Proceedings of the British Academy, 40 (1954), 119-44.

_____ ed., Sir Gawain and the Green Knight, 2nd edition (Oxford, 1967).

Forsström, G., "The Verb 'To Be' in Middle English: a Survey of the Forms", Lund Studies in English, 15 (Lund, 1948).

Foucard, B., A Cathedral Manuscript: I. Westminster Cathedral Chronicle, 50 (1956), 41-3.

Glasscoe, M. ed., Julian of Norwich: A Revelation of Love (University of Exeter, 1976). [Sl]

Grieve, H.E.P., Examples of English Handwriting 1150-1750 (Essex, 1954).

Harford, D., trans., Comfortable Words for Christ's Lovers (London, 1911). [A]

Hodgson, P., ed., Deonise Hid Divinite, EETS OS 231 (London, 1955).

_____ ed., The Cloud of Unknowing and the Book of Privy Counselling, EETS OS 218 (London, 1958).

Horstmann, C., ed., Yorkshire Writers, 2 vols. (London, 1895-96).

Hudleston, R., trans., Revelations of Divine Love, Shewed to a devout Ankress, by name Julian of Norwich (London, 1927). [Sl]

Jacob, E.F. and Johnson, H.C., The Register of Henry Chichele, Archbishop of Canterbury 1414-1443 (Oxford, 1937).

Jones, C., An Introduction to Middle English (New York, 1972).

Ker, N.R., Medieval Manuscripts in British Libraries I (Oxford, 1960).

Lawlor, J., "A Note on the Revelations of Julian of Norwich", RES, N.S., 2 (1951), 255-8.

McIntosh, A., "The Analysis of Written Middle English", Transactions of the Philological Society (1956), 26-55.

_____ "The Textual Transmission of the Alliterative Morte Arthure", in English and Medieval Studies presented to J.R.R. Tolkien (London, 1962), 231-40.

_____ "A New Approach to Middle English Dialectology", ES, 44 (1963), 1-11.

Meech, S.B., and Allen, H.E., The Book of Margery Kempe, EETS OS 212 (London, 1961).

Migne, J.-P., ed., Patrologiae Cursus Completus. Series Latina (Paris, 1844-55).

Molinari, P., Julian of Norwich: The Teaching of a 14th Century English Mystic (London, 1958).

Moore, S., rev. Marckwardt, A.H., Historical Outlines of English Sounds and Inflections (Ann Arbor, 1963).

Moore, S., Meech, S.B., and Whitehall, H., "Middle English Dialect Characteristics and Dialect Boundaries", University of Michigan Publications, Languages and Literature, 13 (1935), 1-60.

Morris, R., ed., The Prick of Conscience (London, 1863).

_____ ed., Old English Homilies, EETS OS 34 (London, 1868).

Mossé, F., trans. J.A. Walker, A Handbook of Middle English (Baltimore, 1961).

Mustanoja, T.F., A Middle English Syntax, Part I (Helsinki, 1960).

Owen, H.W., "Another Augustine Baker Manuscript", Uitgave van Het Ruusbroec-Genootschap (Antwerp, 1968).

Pantin, W.A., The English Church in the Fourteenth Century (Cambridge, 1955).

Parkes, M.B., English Cursive Book-Hands 1250-1500 (Oxford, 1969).

Parry, G.G., ed., English Prose Treatises of Richard Rolle, EETS OS 20 (London, 1866).

Pepler, C., The English Religious Heritage (London, 1958).

Renaudin, P., Quatre Mystiques anglais (Paris, 1945).

Reynolds, A.M., An Edition of MS Sloane 2499 (Leeds University M.A. thesis, 1947).

_____ "Some Literary Influences in the 'Revelations' of Julian of Norwich", Leeds Studies in English and Kindred Languages, 7/8 (1952), 18-28.

_____, ed., Julian of Norwich: Revelations (Leeds University Ph.D. thesis, 1956). [A,P]

_____, trans., A Shewing of God's Love (London, 1958). [A]

Riehle, W., Studien zur englischen Mystik des Mittelalters unter besonderer Berücksichtigung ihrer Metaphorik, Anglistische Forschungen, 120 (Heidelberg, 1977).

Robinson, F.N., ed., The Works of Geoffrey Chaucer (Cambridge, Mass., 1957).

Rye, W., Carrow Abbey, otherwise Carrow Priory: near Norwich (Norwich, 1889).

Samuels, M.L., "Some Applications of Middle English Dialectology", ES, 44 (1963), 81-94.

_____ "The Dialects of MS Bodley 959", in The Earlier Version of the Wycliffite Bible, ed. C. Lindberg, Stockholm Studies in English, 20 (1969), 329-39.

Shepherd, G., "The Nature of Alliterative Poetry in Late Medieval England", Proceedings of the British Academy, 56 (1970), 57-76.

Sisam, K., Fourteenth Century Verse and Prose (Oxford, 1967).

Sitwell, G., ed., The Scale of Perfection (London, 1953).

Smith, T. and Smith, L.T., ed., English Guilds, EETS OS 40 (London, 1963).

Thouless, R.M., The Lady Julian of Norwich, A Psychological Study (London, 1924).

Tolkien, J.R.R., ed., Ancrene Wisse, EETS OS 249 (London, 1962).

Underhill, E., The Mystics of the Church (London, no date).

_____ ed., The Scale of Perfection by Walter Hilton (London, 1948).

Walsh, J., trans., The Revelations of Divine Love of Julian of Norwich (London, 1961). [P]

_____ Pre-Reformation English Spirituality (New York, 1966).

Warrack, G., trans., Revelations of Divine Love (London, 1901). [Sl]

Weber, R., ed., Biblia Sacra Juxta Vulgatam Versionem, (Stuttgart, 1969).

Windeatt, B.A., "Julian of Norwich and her Audience", RES, N.S., 28 (1977), 1-17.

Wolters, C., trans., Revelations of Divine Love (Harmondsworth, 1966). [Sl]

MIDDLE ENGLISH TEXTS

VOLUMES PUBLISHED SO FAR

1   Oliver S.Pickering, *The South English Nativity of Mary and Christ* (1975), 117 pp., DM 24.-

2   Norman F.Blake, *Quattuor Sermones* (1975), 100 pp., DM 24.-

3   John Norton-Smith and Imogen Pravda, *The Quare of Jelusy* (1976), 92 pp., DM 24.-

4   Manfred Görlach, *An East Midland Revision of the South English Legendary* (1976), 123 pp., DM 24.-

5   Walter Sauer, *The Metrical Life of Christ* (1977), 127 pp., DM 29.-

6   Phyllis Moe, *The Middle English Prose Translation of Roger d'Argenteuil's Bible en français* (1977), 111 pp., DM 32.-

7   Diane Bornstein, *The Middle English Translation of Christine de Pisan's Livre du corps de policie* (1977), 224 pp., DM 64.-

8   Frances Beer, *Julian of Norwich's Revelations of Divine Love. The Shorter Version* (1978), 102 pp.

IN PREPARATION

Richard F.S.Hamer, *Three Legends from the Gilte Legende*

Frances McSparran, *Octavian Imperator*

Christina von Nolcken, *The Middle English Translation of the Rosarium Theologie*

CARL WINTER · UNIVERSITÄTSVERLAG · HEIDELBERG